SOTHIS PRESS

Sothis Press aims to completely reimagine the public domain book with an emphasis on universal access to captivatingly designed print editions. We believe that technology will enable every single book ever published to be perpetually accessible in beautiful print form. Sothis is beauty in ubiquity.

www.sothis.press
1 Waterhouse Square, London, ECIN 2ST

The Book of Birmingham

John R. Hornady

SOTHIS PRESS

ISBN 978-1-0368-0125-0

The Book of Birmingham
is in the public domain.

This edition is published by
Sothis Press © 2023. The company
is registered in England and Wales.
The Company Number is 14900389.

FIRST AVENUE, LOOKING EAST

THE BOOK OF BIRMINGHAM

BY

JOHN R. HORNADY

ILLUSTRATIONS BY

W. PAUL PIM

FRONTISPIECE BY

RODERICK D. MACKENZIE

NEW YORK
DODD, MEAD AND COMPANY
1921

CONTENTS

CHAPTER		PAGE
I	In the Beginning	1
II	When Everybody Voted	19
III	The "Double-Cross" in the Seventies	31
IV	Courting the Bauble Fame	44
V	Iron and Steel to the Rescue	56
VI	Roy Cohen's Negro Quarter	68
VII	Visions of Beauty	86
VIII	The People at Play	100
IX	Grave and Gay in Politics	114
X	Turning Ore into Ships	130
XI	Conserving the Human Element	145
XII	Iron for the Confederacy	161
XIII	Popularizing the Water Wagon	179
XIV	The Sway of King Cotton	197
XV	Blazing New Trails	213
XVI	Reforming the Public Dollar	228
XVII	Routing the Reluctant Germ	240
XVIII	Freaks of Fretful Nature	255
XIX	The Teeth of a Child	270
XX	Aladdin's Lamp Surpassed	283
XXI	Far-Flung Influences	299
XXII	Whetting the Intellect	315
XXIII	A City of Ex-Executives	328
XXIV	The Snake-Charmer Eclipsed	346
XXV	Combining Loans with Laughter	363

ILLUSTRATIONS

First Avenue, looklng East . . . . . *Frontispiece*

FACING PAGE

Wire Mill: Recreation, beauty, utility 24
Concrete work in mine 36
Children of the mines perform 48
By-product coke ovens: Plant in background . . 60
The sky line: Red Mountain in the background . . 76
A vista from Red Mountain 92
Where children make merry — City Park . . . 106
A view from the Highlands 120
Steamship fabricated in Birmingham 136
Homes of miners in modern village 152
Modern pig iron plant 168
Homes on the mountainside 186
World's largest rotary coal pump 204
World's largest lake of pitch 204
Underground electric railway 218
Typical South side homes 232
Central hospital, Tennessee Company 246
School and club house in mining village 262
By-product plant. Naval air craft just leaving . . 290
Limestone, ore and coke furnace 306
Science Hall, Birmingham Southern College . . . 320
Two views from the sky. Terminal station in center of lower picture 336
Civic Centre, Fairfield 354
Rear view of Highland homes 368

·PIM·

THE BOOK OF BIRMINGHAM

CHAPTER I

IN THE BEGINNING

THE stupendous assurance of those adventurons spirits who founded the town of Birmingham half a century ago is the most amazing thing about the beginning of this, the South's most populous post-bellum community.

With a series of indifferent farms to start with, they planned a vast metropolis. The sky and the horizon were their limits, and they laid the foundations accordingly.

If one can visualize a long and tortuous valley, traversed by meandering streams which left their banks and wandered far afield whenever the rains descended, one can appreciate something of the faith as well as the vision of the men to whom the city of today owes its being. Were you or I to found a city doubtless we should conclude that it would be a good idea to keep its feet out of the mud. But not so with these men. They knew where they wanted the city, and the fact that its people would have to fight their way to success through seas of liquid earth hindered them no whit. Perhaps they reasoned that the deeper the mud the quicker the paving would materialize. At any rate, they went forward with their plans. And with what magnificence they did their work! With them every gesture was a full-arm movement.

In that valley where stood a single blacksmith shop, they laid out a colossus; a city whose dream streets echoed to the traffic of a vast metropolis and whose fanciful squares were filled with towering structures where vibrated the restless pulse of giants in action.

There were no railroads to serve the commerce in this city, no traffic for streets, no furnaces nor factories nor buildings of whatsoever kind to grace the splendid squares. But these pioneers foresaw the coming of all these things and they demonstrated the sublime character of their faith by the divine excellence of their work.

Hence it is that Birmingham, entering into its own as one of the great industrial centers of the world, has no such problems as confront those all too numerous American cities which grew haphazard along irregular highways and by-ways, to find too late that streets and avenues, which served well enough in the days of the ox-cart, are wholly inadequate to accommodate the traffic of a twentieth century metropolis.

For the vision which gave Birmingham wide thoroughfares, its people should ever be grateful. It was a stroke of genius that should immortalize the men who could visualize a city where stood a lonely shack.

In what was to be the business section of this dream city, they laid out a great checker-board, streets running toward the hills and avenues paralleling the valley. Later they approached the hills and there performed new marvels. Following the contour of Red Mountain on the South, an avenue was designed that for years has ranked among the most wonderful thoroughfares in America. Winding in and out and doubling back at times, it presents an ever changing vista that is a source of lasting joy to home folks and a delightful surprise to every visitor. Flanked by handsome residences, and well groomed lawns, and arched by beautiful trees, Highland Avenue ranks among the really great thoroughfares of the world, and there are others! Becoming more ambitious, the builders of Birmingham pushed their serpentine highways to the very crest of the mountain, and as one traverses these swift ascending avenues he is treated to a magnificent view of the great panorama stretched out in the valley below. Upon the crest of Red Mountain these avenues twine in and out and present vistas such as thrill the artist soul. Those who enter the city below under the impression that it is a mining camp are fairly staggered by the beauty and charm of these highways and by the evidence on every hand of a delightful home life.

But this is getting a long way ahead of the story, and we should leave the asphalt of today and return for a little while to the mud of yesteryear if we would learn something of the characteristics of the town in its beginning. Tough! Birmingham was all of that. No sooner had the far-seeing pioneers who laid the foundations of the city gotten the community under way than adventurous spirits were attracted from the far corners of the earth, and here were enacted just such scenes as were witnessed in the mining camps of California during the great gold rush. Came liquor, came liquor consumers. Came guns and men who knew how to use them. Came a little law and much lawlessness, and came the time when the new-born city attained a national reputation, not so much for the magnitude of its natural resources as for the carelessness with which many of its adventurous citizens handled their weapons. "Bad Birmingham" is the title the city won, and it was by this title that it became known far and wide.

The boom spirit was at its height, with speculation running rife and the gambling fever permeating the very atmosphere. Men rushing about eager to turn a dazzling profit over night had no time for judicial procedure when friction arose. Fights and fatalities were numerous. Speculation and gambling put much money in circulation and crooks came in who got theirs at the point of a revolver. Discreet men in going homeward at night took the middle of the street. Alley corners offered too much danger from the lurking thug.

Stock exchanges had been established and here holdings of all kinds were traded in, stock in boom companies being a favorite offering. In the midst of the excitement, a firm from New Orleans came in and opened an all-night café, where liquors flowed as freely as in any Parisian establishment of its kind. Birmingham ceased to sleep, and the morning paper carried the story of some night-time tragedy in almost every issue.

But these violent expressions of a turbulent spirit were largely surface. The real men of the community, the men who were here to do a man's work because there was a man's job at hand, brought with them the idealist's conception of justice and equity and morals. They held the strong man's contempt for the lurking thug and the cowardly assassin, and gradually the spirit of lawlessness broke its wings against the granite of their character. Came the time when the last man-killer was exiled or hanged or imprisoned, when the last brothel was wiped out, when the last gilded palace of cock-tails, cards and crookedness went by the board.

The swing of the pendulum was far. From being a very bad town, Birmingham became an exception among American cities in wholesome observance of the decencies of life. Here the saloons went long before national prohibition became a fact. Here was built up a religious and moral sentiment which today finds expression in a demand for clean amusements, in churches that are filled on Sabbath morning, in men's Sunday School classes that run into the hundreds, and in a firm insistence upon law enforcement.

That Birmingham has grown in beauty, in intelligence, in morals and in religion as it has grown industrially and commercially is one of the most outstanding facts about the community.

Birmingham has year after year the largest Bible Training School in the world, and it was here that the movement for training schools of this character, now nation-wide, received its initial impetus.

It was in Birmingham that the Laymen's Missionary Movement was made electrical, the first great convention being held in this city. Moreover, there is substantial foundation for the claim that Birmingham gave to prohibition much of the impetus which finally swept the nation into the dry column. In other words, the reform of Birmingham seems to have been just about as complete as such reforms get to be, and the measure of her goodness furnishes an excellent idea of the size her aching head must have been when she raised her right hand to high heaven, after one of those old orgies, and solemnly exclaimed "Never again!"

Another thing that might be said of Birmingham: in spite of its hectic record in the early days, there has never been a lynching in this community, nor has it known the turmoil of a race riot, though forty per cent of its population is colored.

The only serious attempt to lynch a person in this city was made by a white mob which sought the life of a white prisoner. And it was a dark and tragic hour, yet pregnant with the germ of lasting peace.

The prisoner whose life was sought by this mob

was Dick Hawes, who had killed his wife and two children that he might be free to marry again. After the commission of the crime, he did marry, and was on his wedding tour when apprehended and jailed in Birmingham.

Indignation over the brutal and cold-blooded crime was universal, and the crowd which marched to the jail expected to get the prisoner without formidable resistance, as so many mobs had succeeded in doing on similar occasions in other Southern communities. But the blunder which led the gallant Six Hundred to slaughter was not greater than the blunder of those who stormed the jail, for the sheriff who defended it had a rare conception of the meaning of the oath he had assumed. He believed the oath meant what it said and he governed himself accordingly. The shots he poured into that wildly excited mass of humanity were real and were meant to kill, and they did kill. They killed members of the storming party, and more. They killed forever the mob spirit in Birmingham.

In due time Hawes was tried, convicted and hanged, and this orderly procedure has been the fixed rule in handling criminals from that day to this.

The sheriff who put an end to mob violence by his drastic action upon this occasion was Joseph

Smith, popularly known as "Little Joe Smith." His course subjected him to much abuse, and for a time he was in danger of personal violence at the hands of some hot-headed citizens, but when the community had recovered from the shock occasioned by the fact that several prominent citizens, who were mere spectators, were either killed or wounded, the attitude of the public altered, and in after years he was given credit for having done a good work in letting it be known that men charged with crime would be protected, and that attempts to impede the orderly processes of the law were fraught with great danger.

There was something fresh and boyish and exuberant about that little coterie of men who founded Birmingham. While they were in dead earnest about building a city in the valley of their selection, they had a keen sense of humor. They did not take themselves nor their job too seriously. For confirmation consider their attitude toward the rough shack in which they lived while surveys were being made for the city that was tucked away in the back of their heads. Built of rough pine boards, nailed upright upon rough timbers, this long, low shack was dubbed the St. Nicholas Hotel, receiving this title because no name more high-sounding suggested itself. Until the coming of real hotels, this establishment housed a group of men who afterward became famous in the annals of the community.

Prior to the opening of this temporary refuge, the only hotel accommodations available were in Old Elyton, then the county site, some two miles from the new town. Of these hotels, Colonel James R. Powell, the moving spirit in the founding of the new city, and who afterwards became known as "The Duke of Birmingham," dropped this pertinent observation: "They are like the roads in Arkansas, whichever one you take you wish to h— you had taken the other."

It was at one of these ancient hotels in Elyton that Major James Thomas, after whom the great Thomas furnaces are named, stepped upon first entering the valley. He was suffering from a severe headache at the time and told the negro boy to bring him a cup of hot tea. The negro reported presently with an evil looking brew that was so suggestive of lye that Mr. Thomas asked:

"What in the world is this? I told you to get me tea."

"Boss, that's tea," said the negro in a tone which indicated that he had rather a poor opinion of the gentleman's power of perception.

"Well, what kind of tea is it?" asked Mr. Thomas.

"Sassafras tea," replied the darky.

"Take it away," exclaimed Mr. Thomas, "I want real tea and no cheap imitation."

"Then why didn't you say you wanted store-bought tea," exclaimed the boy in fretful tones, "and I'd a done gone and got it for you!"

In those days "store-bought" tea was a luxury in this isolated valley, and such as trickled in had come a weary distance. The Panama Canal, destined to bring the Eastern world thousands of miles nearer to the New, was then no more than a subject of desultory conversation, and it did not enter into the minds of the founders of Birmingham that one day the East would be drawn so near their young city, nor did they realize the tremeudous significance such a development would have upon the community. They builded better than they knew, for today the buyer from the under world who comes to market through the Panama Canal must pass Birmingham long before he can reach any other center where the products of a great industrial community are available. In locating their little shop to catch the trade of the world, these pioneers placed it where the Eastern and the Southern buyer would have to go much farther if they passed their open door, after coming into the Atlantic.

It is doubtful also if the founders of Birmingham realized the full significance of the fact that the city was planted within thirty miles of the Warrior River, a stream impossible for navigation at that time and which few dreamed would some day become the means of conveying Birmingham products to the ends of the world. Today Birmingham has a port upon this stream and tea coming in from China or steel going out to Japan, may go all the way by water. Because of this fact, Birmingham enjoys a water rate, just as if the river flowed through the heart of the city.

The first real hotel erected in Birmingham was known as the Relay House, not because its guests slept in relays, as became the custom at some hotels during the boom, but because of its proximity to the railroads, which by this time had pushed their way into the town. Early registers of this hotel, still in existence, contain the names of many great figures in the financial and industrial world, who came from time to time to see for themselves how much of fact and how much of fiction was contained in the widely published stories of Birmingham's natural wealth.

The rush for the new town was under way before adequate accommodations could be provided, and small hotels and rooming houses sprang up on all sides. Some of these contained large "wards" in which numerous beds were crowded, and it was the usual custom to pull one set of guests out early in the morning in order that others, who had been waiting around all night, might get some sleep. Thus the beds were made to do double duty while the thrifty landlord waxed prosperous.

To the enterprise of the management of one of these early hotels was due the first sidewalk laid in Birmingham. David Bridges, who after a lapse of fifty years still stands behind a Birmingham hotel register, found that the guests of 1872 were a bit hesitant about coming to his hotel on account of the sea of mud that oozed between its hospitable portals and the shack which did duty as a depot, put down a three-foot walk to meet the whims of this element. The walk was held to a width of three feet on account of the excessive cost of lumber, and was in no sense a vote of confidence in the ability of the guests to always walk the straight and narrow path.

In the absence of railroad transportation, the gentlemen who created Birmingham on paper had considerable difficulty in getting a substantial start toward the realization of their aspirations, since lumber and brick are essential factors in city building. However, they found two brick manufacturers who were willing to establish plants in the community if guaranteed an output of a million bricks each, and thereupon a bold policy was adopted. It was determined that no building less than two stories should be erected in the main business district, and that these buildings must be of brick. Not only so, but it was stipulated that all purchasers of business lots should be required to build within twelve months.

Thus the problem of building material was solved by making brick contracts, and the sale of the brick was assured by rigid restrictions as to time and material. That is to say, the problem was solved if the tiny segments of farm land these pioneers had platted and called "lots" could be sold, which was a matter of sheer speculation at the time. When certain of these lots, measuring fifty by one hundred feet, actually were sold for as much as one hundred dollars each, one old-timer was heard to remark that he knew of no speculation that equaled buying farms by the acre and selling them by the foot. His admiration for the genius of the men who could put over such a thing was boundless, but he had a very poor opinion of those who surrendered good money for the lots.

The land that brought this seemingly preposterous price as "city property" was bought from the native farmers on a basis of $25 in cash for two-thirds of their holdings, and $50 in stock for the remaining one-third. Four thousand acres were bought upon this basis, and the stock involved became the foundation of numerous fortunes, as it grew in value at a most astonishing rate with the development of the city. In fact the story of the dividend payments of that pioneer organization, known as the Elyton Land Company, has all the elements of a Jules Verne romance. From $100, those lots leaped into the thousands within a few years, and many small investors found themselves possessed of undreamed wealth.

But it would be erroneous to imagine that this golden stream of wealth flowed in at once or that its course was uninterrupted. It was not all smooth sailing with those bold architects of an industrial empire. They received their bumps. Yea, verily!

Chartered in December, 1871, the new town grew with extraordinary rapidity, and its promoters decided that the time was ripe for a great ingathering. To this end a campaign remarkable both in its boldness and its ingenuity was launched; this with a view to holding a great sale of lots on June 17, 1873.

Colonel Powell had all the genius of the old-time circus promoter when it came to exploitation, and one of his master strokes was to invite the New York Press Association to meet in Birmingham in connection with the Alabama Press Association, which had been induced to come here. He urged the wonders of the new town with such eloquence that a number of New York correspondents actually were sent to investigate its possibilities. They were astonished at the absence of anything that looked like a city, but were profoundly impressed by the show of coal and iron, and they sent back glowing stories of Birmingham's natural resources.

Following this an intensive advertising campaign was adopted, the story of its material wealth being carried to all parts of the United States and to the Old World as well. After months of such exploitation, the promoters succeeded in creating widespread interest in their enterprise, and the outlook appeared most propitious. But just as the dream of an immense throng and an immense sale of lots was about to be realized, the heavens became overcast and presently nature was engaged in giving a fine imitation of the flood which sent Noah scurrying to the Ark. It rained for several weeks and such transportation facilities as existed, limited at best, were so interrupted that it became necessary to call off the sale. This was bump No. 1, and, alas, the worst was yet to come.

In July, 1873, cholera, which had appeared at several points in the South, invaded the town of Birmingham and withered it, not so much because of the ravages of the disease as because of the wildly exaggerated reports that were circulated.

"Birmingham wiped out" was a familiar headline, and it took the community years to recover from the injurious effects.

Swift upon the heels of this disaster came the Jay Cooke panic, the baleful effects of which were being felt throughout the nation in the fall and winter of 1873.

These staggering disasters left many empty houses in Birmingham and many hearts were sick, but hope and faith and the purpose to achieve survived. Having put their hands to the plow, the little group which had planted the town refused to turn back. There is nothing finer in the annals of community building than the courage with which they fought to make good their promises to the world. Neither floods, nor plague, nor panic could shake their purpose, and in the midst of those dark and troublesome times they created a legacy that has become priceless with the passing of the years. Birmingham had been founded upon material things, a body corporate destined to wealth. Now came the spiritual being, fully endowed with the attribute of faith, hope and love; the last a by-product of disaster. The fellowship of trouble knit together those who remained to fight the battles of Birmingham, and here was born a spirit of democracy, the impress of which is manifest today in the fact that the only aristocracy existing in the community is the aristocracy of personal worth. Snobbishness, that colorless product of idleness, has not taken root here. The pace has been too swift.

CHAPTER II

WHEN EVERYBODY VOTED

POLITICS, that great national sport, invaded Birmingham at the very beginning, and forthwith became distinguished for lurid achievements. The first election, held when the new town was less than a year old, attracted people from a radius of a hundred miles, and the privilege of the ballot was freely conferred. People from Montgomery and intermediate points on the South, and Decatur and intermediate points on the North, marched up to the ballot box and voted their preference on a purely local question!

The burning issue on that July day in 1872 was the proposed removal of the county court house from Elyton, the ancient county site, to Birmingham, the infant prodigy. The old settlers, the real natives of the county, constituted a formidable majority. Many of them looked upon the "doings and carryings on" in the new town with thinly disguised suspicion, while the calmness and conservatism of the ancient community in which the court house stood held an irresistible appeal.

Realizing that the tide was flowing against them, the resourceful gentlemen behind the new town decided to meet the situation by giving an immense barbecue on election day, "with an abundance of good things to eat and drink, and with music and other features galore," as the widespread invitations phrased it. Construction trains were brought into service on the morning of the election and hundreds of negro laborers were hauled to town, as were large groups of white people.

The barbecue was spread on the site donated by the land company for the location of the court house, and a huge ballot box was placed close at hand. Brewer's Band, a hastily constructed musical aggregation thrown together by W. P. Brewer, who today is one of the few survivors of that hectic period, discoursed music that made up in volume what it lacked in harmony, and this, with the speech-making, the games and contests, and other feats, made a most thrilling event. Colonel Powell, the "Duke of Birmingham," appeared on the scene attired in royal fashion, his costume adding much to the color of the occasion.

Adorned with a red sash, an army coat which might have been worn by a brigadier general, and wearing a glittering sword, he made an imposing figure. Shortly after he appeared upon a proud-stepping steed, the word spread among the negroes that he was General Grant, who only a few years before had stricken the shackles from the limbs of the black man.

History does not record who was responsible for the rumor that Colonel Powell was General Grant, nor is it known who passed the word among those negroes that the General wanted them to vote to remove the court house to Birmingham as an evidence of their appreciation of what he had done for them in conferring the blessing of freedom, but the impression got out, the word was passed, and forthwith all doubt about how the colored folks would vote melted into thin air. They voted solidly for removal, following an eloquent address by the "General." A rare genius was Colonel Powell, and one acquainted with his sense of humor, his daring, his initiative and his bigness of heart, can but deplore the fact that disappointment dogged his footsteps and tragedy marked the close of his spectacular career.

It was by these methods that the court house was moved from Elyton to Birmingham; methods made possible by legislation enacted under the "carpet-bag" rule which prevailed in Alabama for a number of years following the enfranchisement of the negroes and the disfranchisement of a large part of the white citizenship. Under these laws any one claiming the right to vote could so do, and to challenge this alleged right was to make one liable for prosecution on the charge of obstructing the ballot. Thus the alien voters got away with it. The methods resorted to by the Birmingham boomers on this occasion were the subject of much acrimonious criticism, but the result stood and in due course the court house was removed. Then came the time when the wisdom of the step was conceded universally, and bitterness disappeared. Thus Time, the great healer, condoned the methods of the ward healer.

It might be observed in passing, that the opposition on this occasion also had a few unique strings to its bow. For instance, a brass band that had been imported from Montgomery to assist in the festivities, was composed of men who were careless enough to lay their instruments aside for a little while, only to find upon their return that someone had poured tar into the horns! Yes, it was a lively contest, the forerunner of many other hard fought and spectacular political battles.

Colonel Powell was the second mayor of Birmingham, the first, R. H. Henley, having been appointed by the Governor, but several years later, when he attempted again to attain this honor, he met a most humiliating defeat. His opponent on this occasion was a railroad engineer, and when the latter won after a most turbulent struggle, the Colonel felt his defeat so keenly, that he bade farewell to the city of his dreams and went to Mississippi, where in 1883 he was shot to death in a tavern near Yazoo. Thus ended the career of a Virginian who came to Alabama in his youth, and who played a highly useful part in the development of the State and in the founding of what is now the State's chief city.

The loose political methods which marked the initial struggle in Birmingham continued for a good many years with varying degrees of intensity. No one thought anything of flim-flamming the negro out of his vote during the fervid days of reconstruction, and by easy stages the point was reached when many ardent partisans counted it a shrewd thing, when by some adroit maneuver at the polls, they could defeat the opposition, although the only issue might be: Which element among the whites should be in control. As an illustration of the means adopted in some instances, may be chronicled the story of a once widely known politician whose services were always greatly in demand as an election official. Speaking of a turbulent contest over a quarter of a century ago, he said, "I was one of the clerks at the City Hall box, and during the day I marked a large number of ballots and slipped them under my vest, where they fitted snugly. That evening, when the polls closed, and the ballot box was opened preparatory to beginning the count, I leaned far over the box, pretending to want something on the other side of the table, and at the same moment lifted my vest, spilling the surreptitious ballots down among the others." He thought it a rich joke, and did not hesitate to tell about it in after years. And there are others of this kind, gifted with similar ingenuity.

Coincident with this attitude of semi-indifference to the sacredness of the ballot, there flourished a like indifference to certain niceties in the management of public affairs, such as have come to be observed during the past fifteen or twenty years, partly as a result of quickened public conscience and partly as a result of rigid legislative restrictions.

The aldermanic system thrived here, as in most American cities, and for many years every selfish interest had its representatives on the governing board, and the thing was accepted as a matter of course. The saloons were a large factor in the political life of the community and as a rule sev-

WIRE MILL: RECREATION, BEAUTY, UTILITY

eral saloon keepers were numbered among the aldermen. The old rolling mill district, where Secretary Davis, of President Harding's Cabinet, began his climb toward distinction, was thus represented. Contractual relations with the city were formed by public officials, and city patronage was enjoyed by firms having members in the official family, and little or no attention was paid to such matters. That abuses were not more general is due to the fact that, as a rule the governing body was composed of a majority of men whose purposes were unselfish.

This matter of city officials having business relations with the municipality rocked along until 1905, when a political convulsion thrust a veritable Teddy Roosevelt into the mayor's office in the person of George Ward, who enjoyed what in those days was a rare distinction, in that he was born in Birmingham. Ward put through what was known as an "Anti-graft" ordinance, under which the loose and questionable practices of former years were made unlawful. At the same time he created a great sensation by publicly charging a member of the board of police commissioners with having an interest in a famous dive known as the Rabbit Foot Saloon, and, when the police commissioners failed to act in the matter, he caused the offending official to be impeached before the board of aldermen.

On one occasion, when the aldermanic board became arrayed against Ward and elected a presiding officer who sought to usurp the duties of that office, Ward beat the "pretender" to the chair, and, slapping a large and formidable looking revolver upon the desk, announced that he was at the helm and was going to remain there. And he did.

It happened that President Roosevelt visited Birmingham while Ward was mayor, and the latter, given to few words as a rule and being anything but an orator, decided to distinguish himself in his welcome address to the President. To this end he wrote a speech full of beautiful and well rounded sentences, and spent weary hours memorizing it. At last the great day arrived and with it the President. Ward, with a large number of other prominent citizens, met the train. There was a vast throng present, and, as the Colonel stepped out upon the platform, a mighty cheer went up from the multitude.

At this crucial moment, Mayor Ward raised his voice and exclaimed, "Mr. President." Then he stopped, thought for a moment, and started over again. "Mr. President." A pause, then the Mayor ceased to struggle with his fugitive memory and proceeded: "Mr. President, I had a fine speech of welcome for you, but I've forgotten every word of it, but we are glad to have you as our guest."

The broad grin for which the Colonel was famous, became pronounced at this juncture, and reaching for the hand of Ward, he exclaimed: "Mr. Mayor, that's the finest speech I've heard since I left Washington!"

Roosevelt, by the way, was very popular in Birmingham, and no-where was his famous joke about "Why I'm a Democrat" more enjoyed. The joke, as told here, ran something like this:

A Northerner and a Southerner were discussing matters political in the smoking compartment of a Pullman, when the Northerner asked:

"Why is it that you men of the South are practically all Democrats? In the North we divide; there you will find Republicans, Democrats, Progressives, Independents, and so forth, while you of the South stick together in the Democratic party. Why is this? Why, for instance, are you a Democrat?"

"Well," drawled the Southerner, "my father was a Democrat, my grandfather was a Democrat and my great-grandfather was a Democrat, so, of course, I'm a Democrat."

"Ah," said the Northerner, "suppose your

father had been a horse-thief and your grandfather had been a horse-thief and your great-grandfather had been a horse-thief, what would you have been then?"

"Oh, I guess in that case I'd have been a Republican," was the reply of the Southerner, according to the widely smiling Colonel.

Another President who enjoyed visiting Birmingham was Mr. Taft, and on one of his brief stays here, he performed a little act of thoughtfulness that did much to endear him to the people. He was being escorted to the Country Club, where a dinner was to be tendered him, and while on the way, he turned to one of the gentlemen in the automobile in which he was riding, and asked: "Doesn't Rufus Rhodes live out this way somewhere?"

"Yes," was the reply.

"Then please have the car run by his house."

The car was stopped and the occupants of the other automobiles, constituting a somewhat lengthy procession, were told to drive on to the Club. Thereupon the car containing the President was run around to the residence of Mr. Rhodes, who was desperately ill and who died shortly thereafter. There Mr. Taft left the car, and, mounting the steps, he rang the bell and asked for Mrs. Rhodes. When she appeared, he inquired about the condition of Mr. Rhodes and expressed his sympathy in terms of deep sincerity.

General Rhodes was editor and founder of the "Birmingham News," one of the leading Democratic papers of the South, but he was a great admirer of Taft, and this admiration led him to make a speech at Augusta, Georgia, which caused a gale of laughter to sweep the country and for which he was twitted no little by his colleagues of the Democratic faith. He had gone to Augusta, where Mr. Taft was spending his vacation, to speak for a delegation that wished to invite the President to Birmingham, and in the course of his speech he made the statement that, during the preceding Presidential election, "We voted for Bryan, but prayed for Taft." It amused Taft greatly, but as much could not be said of Bryan, and from that time forward there was a coolness between the Commoner and the Editor, such as had not prevailed theretofore.

How narrowly General Rhodes missed going to the United States Senate as a successor to Senator John T. Morgan, and the amazing piece of political maneuvering by which this culmination was defeated, forms a story that is without a parallel in the political history of America.

Both Senator Morgan and Senator Pettus, who had represented Alabama in the United States

Senate for many years, were far advanced in age by 1900, and it was realized that they could not survive for many more years. Therefore the minds of the politically inclined began to turn upon the matter of their successors.

B. B. Comer had been elected Governor after a sensational fight for railroad regulation, and it was the general opinion that if either of the venerable senators should pass away, he would appoint Rhodes to the vacancy. Those in charge of the Democratic machinery in the State were bitterly opposed to this, and in order to take the matter out of the hands of the Governor, they evolved the unprecedented plan of holding a primary election to elect successors to Morgan and Pettus while these gentlemen were alive and actively on duty in Washington. In this election, which became known as "the post-mortem primary," John H. Bankhead, who had just been defeated for Congress by Captain Richmond P. Hobson, and Ex-Governor Joseph F. Johnston, received the nomination. Thus any chances Rhodes might have had went glimmering and, in due course, both Bankhead and Johnston went to the Senate.

CHAPTER III

THE "DOUBLE-CROSS" IN THE SEVENTIES

WHILE black slaves bent their backs to the task of building the railroad that was destined first to enter the great mineral section of Alabama, controversy upon the question of human chattels raged the nation over, and before this road was finished controversy gave way to armed conflict, and, pending the issue, constructive works hung in suspense. From the task of building this railroad, the slaves were called back to farm and plantation, there to exert every ounce of strength in producing food and clothing for men at war. Commerce could wait until the War God had his feast!

This early railroad enterprise, which was designed to run to Chattanooga from a point on the Mobile & Ohio Railroad near Meridian, passing through the coal and iron fields of Alabama, had its inception at a barbecue given in a grove at Elyton, (now part of Birmingham) in the summer of 1854.

At that time stage coaches, each drawn by six horses, ran from Elyton to Huntsville, on the North, and to Montgomery, on the South. These coaches provided the only regular means of transportation for individuals, and offered no hope as a means of transporting such materials as existed in the mineral district. In order to stimulate interest in a plan he had conceived for bringing a railroad into the district, Col. William S. Ernest arranged a great barbecue at Elyton and invited men of influence from all parts of the State.

In those days the barbecue was an even greater institution than at this time. In many communities it was the most notable event of the year, looked forward to with the liveliest interest, and always the occasion of a great outpouring. It meant an incomparable feast, for there were no other means known for giving to meat the appetizing quality it acquired when roasted above hot coals, being drenched the while with sauces that imparted a rare and delectable flavor.

Before the day of the barbecue, great trenches were dug, and into these was piled the oaken fuel. Across the trenches iron racks were laid, upon which the beef and mutton and pork and poultry, and deer and bear and wild turkey, were placed for roasting. Then, early in the morning of the great day, the fires were lighted, and for hours the meats would roast, every piece being watched by men skilled in the art of out-door cooking. Brunswick stew, a famous Southern dish, would be brewing in huge pots, while in scores of homes, near and far, dainties of a special fineness would be in course of preparation.

For miles and miles the people would come, in every conceivable form of vehicle — fancy buggies, drawn by high-stepping horses; ancient coaches, with high-hatted drivers upon the high front seats; wagons made in the neighboring blacksmith shop; wagons fresh from the factory; carts, with enormous wheels, drawn by enormous oxen. Thus men brought their families, while scores of young fellows appeared astride horses and mules, which they tied in the friendly shade.

Homes were few and far between in those days, and most of these people led a lonely existence. So the barbecue, like the old-time camp-meeting, afforded a point of contact, and was a day luminous in the life of the people. Oratory they had, too, in those days, the real thing. Men did not hesitate to paint the lily nor add luster to the rainbow.

Their souls were full of poetry, and they let it flow, to the vast delight of those assembled throngs.

It was on such an occasion as this that the first railroad project was launched, and one may judge the excellence of the food by the measure of success the promoter attained. A considerable amount of stock was purchased on the spot, and committees were named to see planters all along the proposed route with a view of interesting them in the project. These committees discharged their duties well, inducing many land-owners who could not subscribe in cash, to take stock and pay for it by having their slaves lay so many miles of railroad. It was through this arrangement that the slave labor became such an important factor in pushing the work during its early stages. Thus matters progressed in a very satisfactory manner until the outbreak of the war, when all such activities were brought to an abrupt close.

About the time this railroad, known as the North-East and South-West, was being started, there was considerable agitation in favor of another highway, the dream of its promoters being to link the Tennessee River with the Alabama River, and thus have a railway uniting the mineral section of the State to the two great navigable streams. In 1858, the Legislature appropriated $10,000 for preliminary work on this enterprise, which was called the Alabama Central Railroad. John T. Milner, an aggressive Southerner who had been pioneering in the gold fields of California, was made chief engineer. The vast extent of the mineral resources in North Alabama impressed him profoundly, and in his initial report to Governor Moore he said: "We are at the beginning of the development of gigantic national resources."

It was determined to push on with the enterprise, but a dispute arose between Montgomery and Selma concerning the Southern terminus, and the issue had to be fought out on the floors of the Legislature. Both of these ancient cities stand on navigable streams, and, in those far days, each was jealous of any advantage that might accrue to the other. In the end a compromise was reached under which the new road was brought to a point on the old East Tennessee, Virginia and Georgia Railroad, exactly the same distance from Selma as from Montgomery — a fifty-fifty proposition, as it were. The point of contact was in the woods at that time, but Calera, a town of several thousand people, has since developed there.

Work on this road also was stopped by the war, but, as with the older enterprise, it was resumed after the close of the conflict.

With both of these railroads approaching the future city of Birmingham, and destined to cross at some point in the vicinity, it occurred to Milner that it would be a fine idea for the promoters of the two roads to come to an agreement about the junction point, and then acquire a large amount of land adjacent to the crossing, since a city of considerable proportions was sure to spring up with the development of the coal and iron deposits.

This idea appealed to the moving spirit in the other road, and it was decided to locate the crossing in a valley three or four miles to the North of the present city. Thereupon options were obtained upon several thousand acres of land, and Milner went forward with his road as determined upon in the agreement. Later he learned that the directing head of the other enterprise had changed his plans and, with a view to owning the future city in its entirety, had obtained options upon several thousand acres, constituting the present site of Birmingham, and had routed his road so that the crossing would come upon this property.

This development, which demonstrates that the methods of the frenzied financier were known even in those days, left Milner and his associates with a lot of useless options on their hands, and with hopes of a fortune knocked into nothingness. His associates were dumbfounded by the development, and felt they had been robbed of the best fruits of a most promising enterprise, for all of them were

confident that the city of their dreams would materialize at the crossing, and that the land would become immensely valuable. This, as a matter of fact, is exactly what happened, and they would have had no part in the tremendous increment in values but for the adroit scheme of beating the enemy which developed in the head of Milner.

Without divulging to a single individual, what he had in mind, Milner began to run new surveys far East of those originally made, thus creating the impression that he was going to change the route so that it would cross the other steel highway seven or eight miles above the point where the exclusive options had been obtained. This so disconcerted the moving spirit in the other road that he was afraid to exercise his options, since outright purchase would have involved a large amount of money, and this is just the state of mind that Milner had hoped to create. As a matter of fact, the situation was so uncertain that the options were allowed to expire. They were to have been taken up at a bank in Montgomery by noon of a certain day, but the holder had become so confused by the maneuvers of Milner that he failed to put in an appearance.

In the meantime, Milner had arranged to obtain the same options in the event the enemy failed to close, and he and his friends were on hand with this end in view. When the time came, the options passed into friendly hands. Thereupon the property was purchased, the sum of $100,000 being advanced for this purpose by Josiah Morris, at the solicitation of Milner. Later the property was deeded to the Elyton Land Company, during the corporate life of which it became worth many millions of dollars.

When the enemy had been outwitted in this fashion, Milner resumed construction on his road along the line originally intended, and the location of the future city was fixed. He did not get the city exactly where he had expected to have it, but he and his associates got the land upon which it was to stand — this in spite of the fact that the options were obtained by another, who had gone to the length of changing the route of his road in an effort to become sole owner of the South's future industrial metropolis.

Birmingham today has nine trunk line railroads, representing 32,000 miles of track, and two local railroads which render special service to the district. One of these forms a loop about the city, touching practically all important manufacturing establishments, while the other performs a wider loop and renders a similar service to furnace and mining enterprises throughout the territory. From the latter, scores of spur tracks radiate, going to coal mines, ore mines, quarries, furnaces and similar enterprises. With the nine trunk lines leaving in various directions, and with the loop lines circling the district, a railroad map of Birmingham looks not unlike the web of a giant spider.

For a good many years the city was dependent upon railroad transportation, and its development as a wholesale or jobbing center was hindered somewhat by the fact that some cities in the same general territory enjoyed the advantage of water rates. With a view of meeting this situation, the development of transportation on the Warrior River was urged with tireless persistence, and gradually that stream was deepened through the erection of huge dams, until it became navigable to a point within thirty miles of Birmingham. Thereupon, the Port of Birmingham was established and this city was given a river rate. Now self-propelled steel barges carry Birmingham products to Mobile and New Orleans, where they are transferred to vessels and carried to all parts of the world. The same barges return laden with merchandise for the city of Birmingham, brought much cheaper than it can be shipped by rail. This development, which was made possible by the expenditure of millions of dollars on the part of the government in the improvement of the Warrior

River, is a comparatively new thing, but it promises to play a tremendous part in the future of the city. Birmingham products essentially are heavy, and the fact that these products may now be floated to the Gulf, and there placed upon steamers which ply the seven seas, gives the district an added advantage. Water transportation now furnishes the one thing that has been lacking.

The measure of the revolution wrought in transportation in this district during the fifty years since Birmingham's founding, is difficult to visualize, but one may sense something of its magnitude by recalling the old stage-coach, as it was drawn slowly and toilsomely over the rough mountain roads. Then watch the flight of the huge aircrafts, as they arise from the Dixie Flying Field and, after soaring high in the blue, dart away at a speed of a hundred miles an hour.

Which reminds us that Birmingham is an aerial center of world-wide reputation. Because of the ideal geographical location, and the presence of large quantities of by-product gas of unusual lifting power, this city was chosen as the starting point for the great international balloon race of 1920, in which Belgium carried off the honors. Later, when the selection of an American contender at the Belgium meet was to be made, Birmingham again was chosen, and it so happened that the air-craft that won in this event was "The Birmingham Semi-Centennial." This balloon will represent the United States at the international contest in Belgium, and will be the means of advertising to the Old World the fact that a New World city is celebrating its fiftieth birthday.

Birmingham's street railway system, embracing over two dozen lines, penetrates every part of the city and reaches all adjoining communities of importance. Bus lines are numerous, many of these operating between the city and rural communities over excellent county highways. Jefferson County has hundreds of miles of splendid roads, most of them of chert, but many being paved with asphalt as they approach the city. The far-reaching paving program has been outlined by the county authorities, and continued progress along this line is certain.

In the city proper, there is more than a hundred miles of hard-surface pavement, most of it asphalt upon a concrete base. Tremendous strides are being made in paving the city, the program for this year calling for expenditures of more than a million dollars. Such unpaved streets as remain are in a bad condition as a rule, the hilly nature of the land causing them to wash easily, but all important thoroughfares are being paved as rapidly as the work can be done. In pushing paving with such extraordinary vigor, the municipal government proceeds upon the theory that good streets proclaim a good town. Then an additional incentive is found in the fact that a paved street costs practically nothing to maintain, when the paving is done right, while money spent in improving unpaved streets is so much money laid down for Jupiter Pluvius to wash into storm sewers, which is the last place the city wants it to go.

In this connection, it is interesting to note how time solves so often the problem of waste materials. For years and years huge mountains of refuse, called "slag," accumulated about the furnaces of Birmingham. All the waste material which came out of the ore had to be dumped somewhere, and about every iron-maker there arose a great mountain composed of this material. For years it was nothing more than an expensive nuisance, encumbering the land and presenting an unsightly appearance. Then it developed that out of the slag could be made a high-class road material; that it was even better than crushed stone for making the concrete base with which bituminous roads are provided, and thus a great demand was created. About the same time a process was found for making brick and similar materials out of slag, with the result that the growth of these artificial mountains was halted, and the owners began to get a return on something they thought was a total loss.

The presence of vast quantities of this slag in and about the city, furnishes Birmingham with an inexhaustible supply of road material, since the production of slag will go on so long as iron is made.

For the surface treatment of highways, Birmingham by-product plants produce bituminous materials upon a colossal scale, but the story of the multiplicity of things extracted from coal by these enterprises is told in another chapter.

CHAPTER IV

COURTING THE BAUBLE FAME

THE swollen postal receipts of this city are not due altogether to the stirring commerce, nor yet to the voluminous correspondence incident to the conduct of vast industrial enterprises, for be it known that here the literary urge is persistent and insistent. Writers are numerous, and the distinguished success achieved by the few proves an endless source of inspiration to the many. Hence the stream of manuscripts flowing through the postoffice and hence the fame that now and then descends upon some local genius in the field of literary endeavor.

Birmingham's most distinguished writer is Octavus Roy Cohen, whose books are widely read and who also is known to fame as the author of many short stories depicting the ingenuities and eccentricities of the negro, the scene of these amusing and always interesting escapades being laid in Birmingham. But Cohen's popularity among his home folks is not due to the success he has achieved in the literary field. His sympathetic interest in the aspirations of struggling writers, and his willingness to be of assistance to them, has won for him a place in their hearts that might well be envied by any who rejoice in the affection of their fellows. He is the dean of a group of writers, most of them unknown, whose members meet regularly to hear and discuss the mental products of one another, helpful suggestions being the central thought.

One of the first Birmingham writers to attain the distinction of producing a "best seller" was Mary Johnston, whose "To Have and to Hold," and "Prisoners of Hope," gave her a pre-eminent position among creators of fiction. Unlike Cohen, she left Birmingham a few years after achieving success.

Bozeman Bulger, now on the editorial staff of a great national magazine, is another Birmingham writer known to fame, but no longer a citizen of the community. However, his departure was not altogether volitional. The local newspaper upon which he worked years ago found his stories too indifferent for a modern journal, and so he was set adrift. Thereupon he went to work on a New York paper that was less discriminating, and in a little while his name became known to baseball fans the country over. Then he began writing magazine articles, theatrical skits and so forth, and finally reached his present position.

It may be interesting to Bulger to know that the old boarding house where he and I took our meals in those days when the price of a meal was not always a simple problem, afterwards became a negro boarding house, and then was swallowed up in the maw of commercial progress. I wonder if he remembers the gentleman with the large mustache who used to drink half the contents of the cream pitcher when the back of the landlady was turned, or the large and peevish Chesterfield who arose from his seat one day and knocked the colored waiter across the length of the dining room because of some slight breach of etiquette? The heroes of these incidents are dead, but not so with the young man, no longer young, who used to tell the waiter, "I want five spoonsful of coffee," and who heaped maledictions upon the head of the unhappy negro if the coffee measured more or less than the quantity prescribed. This gentleman is living today and exactness still is his motto. The kind and gentle doctor, who prescribed for our ills, is dead, and the saloon keeper who sat at the head of the table is married, falling victim long ago to the charms of the landlady.

Bulger was not the only newspaper man who lost a job here and found a position elsewhere; the distinction between a job and a position being, as I understand it, that one involves lots of work and little pay, while the other means little work and much pay. Sewell Haggard was set adrift by the paper with which he worked here and, having nothing else to do, he went to New York. There he reached the top in the newspaper field, and then became the editor of a magazine of national circulation.

At this point I feel sure that the reader expects the writer to point some moral from the experience of Bulger and Haggard, but I can only offer the feeble suggestion that perhaps the spark of genius has to be fired before it will flame.

Literary expression in Birmingham has not been confined to prose. Here, too, is many an unsung Milton, or those who would be Miltons. And here has arisen at least one figure whose fame has become widespread. Clement Wood started out to reform the world through the introduction of the Socialistic era, and wound up by penning verses that placed him in the forefront among American producers of the muse. His fame was won after he left Birmingham for New York, but he continued to call this his home and to visit here occasionally. He first leaped into prominence among his home people by reason of the enthusiasm with which, as judge of the police court, he laid up fines against the malefactors of great wealth. Later, when he ran for City Commissioner, he won added favor among the proletarians by the masterly fashion in which he took the hide off the capitalistic class. However, the measure of favor was not sufficient to win preferment, and shortly after the returns were in, he left the city, not to brood or repine, but to convert his reverses into verses. And a good job he made of it. A Paris journal devoted to such topics ranks him as one of the six greatest poets of today.

Frances Nimmo Green, now of Montgomery, began her literary career in Birmingham, where she occupied the position of society editor of a newspaper and gained her first experience in fiction while writing descriptive articles concerning functions and figures in the social realm. "The Devil to Pay," one of her early stories, did not pay to any marked extent, but "The Right of the Strongest" was a great success.

The author of the "Jarr Family" is another writer who once lived in Birmingham but who for a good many years has lived Some-where-on-the-Hudson. Roy McArdle resided here in the hey-

CHILDREN OF THE MINES PERFORM

day of Birmingham's youth and made his contribution to the gaiety of the period, but in those days newspaper work was more frequently rewarded with an order on the grocer than with a check on the bank, and he was inspired to seek pastures new.

Those were hard days in the newspaper profession. Many times I have seen the boys gather around on pay-day while the business manager made his excuses for an almost empty till, and heard them express their choice about the kind of "order" they wanted. The married man usually wanted groceries, and perhaps a pair of shoes for the baby, while the single members of the writing group took theirs in meal tickets and sundry articles of adornment. The newspapers could get advertising to be "traded out," but advertising to be paid for in cash was a scarce article. I have seen Frank O'Brien, one of the pioneer publishers, weep real tears as he deplored the inability of his paper to meet its payrolls. But those times long since have gone, and with their passing there seems also to have passed something that was wonderfully fine; a spirit of sympathetic consideration and of loyal co-operation on the part of employees such as money could not buy. Everybody, printers, pressmen, reporters and solicitors, knew what the "old man" was up against, and made his burdens their own. They loved the "old sheet'' and went hungry for it, and wore their clothing threadbare for it. A fine and loyal crowd it was that laid the foundations upon which the rich and powerful journals of today stand in such security!

Rufus Rhodes, founder of the Birmingham News, was the first publisher in the city to adopt the then startling system of paying his men off in cash when the cash was due, and a right popular shop his became. He also insisted on more business-like arrangements with the advertisers, and gradually order was brought out of the chaos in which the newspaper publishing business was plunged.

Ruth Sharpel McVoy resided in Birmingham when she produced ''The Traitor's Son,'' but inasmuch as her husband, Rev. E. C. McVoy, is a Methodist minister subject to the quadrennial changes imposed by this church, she no longer resides in this city.

A novelist who believes Birmingham a sort of glorified annex to the City Celestial, and who could not be persuaded to leave, as so many writing folks have done, is Mittie Owen McDavid, author of several popular works, including ''Princess Pocahontas,'' and ''Children of the Meadow.'' She, too, has been a guide and mentor to the struggling and has done much to encourage both the production and the appreciation of good literature.

Helen Smith Woodruff, author of "Mr. Doctor Man," and "Lady of the Lighthouse," had her home in Birmingham, and Sidney Lazarus, whose skits are familiar to theatregoers in New York, is a product of this city.

A studious writer, now dead, who impressed his personality upon Birmingham, was John Witherspoon DuBose, author of "General Joe Wheeler and the Army of Tennessee," and a history of Alabama.

Other Birmingham writers whose works have been of much more than local interest include Annie Kendrick Walker, author of "Old Shorter Houses and Gardens;" Gerrad Harris, author of "Trail of the Pearl," and "Treasures of the Land;" Dr. Orien T. Dozier, author of numerous poems relating to the valor of the Confederate soldier, and Ethel Armes, author of "Coal and Iron in Alabama," and other works.

While the literary urge has been more pronounced in Birmingham than the call of the stage, the latter has not gone unheard, as witnessed by the success of Henry Walthall, a Birmingham man, and May Allison and Lois Wilson, Birmingham girls. All of these are stars in the film world. And, speaking of films, reminds me of an incident of a quarter of a century ago that is rather amusing in the light of present day developments.

At that time the silent drama was experiencing a sketchy existence in one or two of the larger cities of the country, about the most thrilling thing being the passing of the Empire State Express. However, some saw in the moving picture a permanent means of entertainment, and "nickel houses" were being opened here and there. About this time Howell Graham began talking to me about the possibilities of such an enterprise in Birmingham, finally persuading himself that the thing was worth trying. But, alas, the procession did not wait, and one day Graham came to me with the doleful intelligence that the local field had been pre-empted — someone had opened a picture house! The idea that two such institutions might survive in a city of thirty thousand people did not occur to him, and he went to Chattanooga to launch his enterprise. Truly the movie has moved, but few could foresee then that it was equipped with super-seven-league boots!

The picture house established here at that time, and which sent Graham scurrying to Chattanooga, was the first to open in the South. The manager had been associated with a man who was operating a house in Pittsburgh, and the success achieved by that experiment prompted him to come to Birmingham, Pittsburgh, as he saw it, not being big enough for another enterprise of this character.

One of the most laughable things ever witnessed in a picture house occurred in the theatre opened by Graham in Chattanooga. Graham saw even then that it would be a tremendous advantage to have some means of keeping his house cool on hot days, and he devised a system of pipes through which air was blown into the house by a fan. These pipes were covered with ice, and the result was highly pleasing. The only trouble was that condensation set in when the fan stopped, and water accumulated in the pipes. To keep this water from being sprayed over the audience, it was the custom to cover the vent with a sack when the fan was started, and keep it there until the interior of the pipes became dry.

In those days the picture producer was dependent upon nature for most of his creations, Charlie and Fatty not having appeared on the scene, and the custard-pie art being in its infancy. As a result, street scenes, railroad scenes and ocean scenes were numerous. It so happened that Graham was showing an ocean scene at the time of this incident, great waves rushing over the rock-bound coast and there dashing themselves to pieces. While this picture was being displayed one afternoon, the darky who looked after the air cooling plant neglected to put the sack over the vent before the fan was started, and the result was startling. A veritable shower was thrown upon the audience, and as one man rushed out he exclaimed: "Marvelously realistic; those waves splashed all over me!"

Graham, by the way, made the first aluminum screen upon which a motion picture was shown. A painter by profession, he conceived the idea that aluminum would bring out the fine points of the picture, and he painted his curtain accordingly. It was a great success, and subsequently he painted similar curtains for other movie men. A year and a half after conceiving this idea he was summoned as a witness in the United States Court, and there found that two rival concerns were fighting over the patent rights to the aluminum screen! The idea, to which he had given scarcely a thought, save as it affected his own playhouse, had become worth a fortune, but not to him. Having neglected to answer any of those alluring patent-attorney advertisements, he had to stand by and see others fight over the spoils. Today he is back in Birmingham, out of the picture business, but furnishing most of the local show houses with posters from his second-story paint-shop.

Not all of Birmingham's talented newspaper writers have been forced to seek other fields by reason of being dropped from the payroll, as the thoughtless might infer from the experience of Bulger and Haggard. Some linger. There is Paul Cook, who conducts a "column," and whose jokes are reproduced in humorous papers all over the country. Though profoundly solemn of countenance, he is recognized as one of the leading newspaper humorists of the country.

Then there is "Dolly Dalrymple," one of the sprightliest writers and cleverest women the city has produced. Putting witty sayings into the mouths of darkies is one of her specialties. "Dolly" is Mrs. Orline Shipman.

Another clever pen-pusher is Frank Willis Barnett, doctor of divinity, lawyer, editor and erstwhile globe-trotter, who writes entertainingly on any and all subjects, and who will make a speech on the slightest provocation.

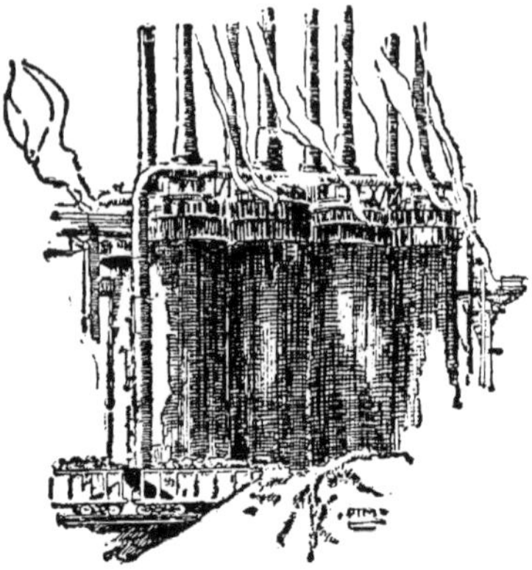

CHAPTER V

IRON AND STEEL TO THE RESCUE

IT is significant that the birth of Birmingham came at a time when activities in the South hung almost in suspense. In this wide and fertile territory vast wealth has been amassed from the soil through the medium of slave labor. Cotton, corn, sugar cane, tobacco and kindred crops grew in abundance and found a ready market. The cost of production was low and the profits generous. Under the circumstances little thought was given to industrial development, and vast deposits of coal, iron, marble and similar products remained untouched.

Then came the war in which the South spent its material resources, pouring the accumulated wealth of generations into the struggle for the

Confederacy, only to lose in the end. With the close of the conflict, slave labor, which had been the backbone of agricultural development, vanished. Thus, with its material accumulation gone, with its labor freed, and its scheme of existence torn to shreds, the South was as a ship without a rudder.

The fight to come back had been on for five years when Birmingham was born, the progress being slow and tedious to a degree that tried the souls of men. And the early come-back was distinctly along agricultural lines. Only the merest handful dreamed of an industrial South. Cotton, the prostrate King, aspired once more to a position of world eminence, and the South's hope was wrapped up in the fulfilment of this aspiration.

But the handful who visioned the South enriched through the development of its mineral wealth looked farther. Then Birmingham was born, and here were laid the deep foundations of an industrial structure that has spread to far places and has become the basis of a new and more permanent form of wealth. And it is rather a gripping fact that today the tonnage of the Birmingham district is greater than that of the entire cotton crop of the South.

The development of the huge deposits of iron and coal in the Birmingham district caused new railroads to push their way into this section, opening up the while vast territories which theretofore had been without transportation facilities. Moreover, these adventures gave a tremendous impetus to the discovery and development of mineral deposits in other parts of the South, with the result that a new era was introduced, and the time came when the South no longer limped upon a single crutch. Rather it strode along to undreamed wealth upon two sturdy limbs, agriculture and industry.

The geographical location of the new city was ideal for communicating this quickened industrial spirit. Placed in the very center of the cotton producing states, and soon equipped with arteries of commerce that penetrated every part of the South, the influence of Birmingham became like that of the leaven which permeated the whole lump.

It all sounds magical, even entrancing, in the telling, but how slow and tedious in the actual achievement, and how fraught with the birth-pains of creative effort!

Despite the bold confidence of that little company of pioneers who planned with such assurance, Birmingham iron did not readily lend itself to the processes of manufacture. Birmingham coal had not yet been transformed into coke, and charcoal was used for fusing the ore. Of this somewhat expensive material it required 196 tons to produce a ton of iron in 1873. The old Oxmoor furnace, operating with charcoal, proved a veritable "white elephant," and the time came when it was taken in satisfaction of a debt for timber — and very poor satisfaction it proved to those who took it. With a debt of $240,000 hanging over it, the owners, desperate and discouraged, finally offered to turn the property over to anyone who would take it and demonstrate that iron could be made successfully in the Birmingham district.

Here was a challenge that startled the community. In the apt colloquialism of the present day, it meant "put up or shut up."

Thus far Birmingham's dream of greatness had been founded upon the fact that she was compassed about by tremendous deposits of coal and iron. With an environment like this, her founders had challenged the world to come and grow rich through the development of these proud possessions. The most glittering claims had been advanced, and upon the basis of these claims a large amount of money had been invested in the community.

Now the founders and builders were face to face with a stern reality. They stood confronted with the cold and clammy truth that it is one thing to possess raw materials and quite another thing to transmute those materials into merchandise that may be exchanged for currency in the markets of the world.

Facing this situation, a little company of moving spirits gathered in the office of the Elyton Land Company with a view to formulating some plan of action, and if they cherished any delusions about the community in which their money had been invested, they left their delusions at the door. They went in for a real diagnosis, realizing that they had reached the parting of the ways and that it was up to them to determine whether Birmingham was to go the way of so many boom towns, or was to come into the heritage they had pictured for it in their hours of optimism, and while they deliberated destiny awaited without!

The meeting, which had been called by Major John T. Milner, was well attended and most of those present were fighting men, veterans of arduous campaigns under Lee, Jackson, Hood, Johnston and other distinguished leaders of the Confederacy. Subsequent events proved that they carried their fighting spirit into the meeting, and to this fact the Birmingham of today owes much of its greatness.

A gentleman by the name of Mudd — Judge W. S. Mudd — was called to the chair, he being for the moment the harassed custodian of the "white

elephant" into which the Oxmoor furnace had developed. Major W. J. Milner acted as secretary, and Colonel John T. Milner, one of the strong props of the struggling community, made the opening address. L. S. Goodrich, an iron expert of considerable reputation, and others, made talks, the burden of which was that Birmingham had to push on and that the only way to do it was to devise some means of converting Birmingham coal into coke and to use this coke instead of charcoal.

Before the meeting adjourned an organization known as the Experimental Coke and Iron Company was formed, and committees were named to solicit subscriptions to carry on the experimental work.

That the flamboyant atmosphere had disappeared from Birmingham as a result of bitter reverses is aptly illustrated by the difference in the name adopted for the company on this occasion and the name of the concern that had gone on the rocks and was ready to turn its property over to anybody or any institution that would run it. The name of the sadly disappointed organization was the Eureka Mining & Transportation Company, a title suggestive of mighty triumphs. The new organization was openly and confessedly "experimental." Birmingham had gotten down to bed-rock.

At a subsequent meeting of this newly formed company a Belgian inventor by the name of Shantle appeared and submitted a coke oven which he claimed was the thing the Birmingham people needed to solve the problem of utilizing their own coal in coke-making. The invention looked promising and shortly thereafter five of the ovens were built under the direction of Captain Frank P. O'Brien, an energetic Irishman who afterwards cut a wide swath in the business and political life of the community.

At this second meeting of the experimental company a committee, which consisted of Ben F. Roden, John T. Milner, Willis J. Milner, W. S. Mudd and Frank P. O'Brien, reported a plan of permanent organization, and upon the adoption of this plan Colonel J. W. Sloss, Charles Linn and W. S. Mudd were constituted the board of managers.

The suspense with which the operation of this experimental organization was watched was akin to that with which members of a family watch at the bedside of a stricken father or mother. The industrial life of the district was at a standstill. The outcome involved not only the future of all iron-making projects, but future railroad projects as well. The South and North, now Louisville & Nashville Railroad, which had been pushed into the district because of the tonnage that seemed so certain in the beginning, was a virtual corpse. There was no tonnage to haul and no passenger traffic to serve. A single passenger car was operated Southward to Calera once a week, and the ghastly truth had dawned upon most every one that unless iron could be produced in the Birmingham district upon a commercial basis this railroad would have to be abandoned, as would every other project of a similar character.

At this time there were only three coal mines in operation in Alabama, but the owners of these were eager to promote the coke-making industry, and they donated coal for experimental purposes. The South & North Railroad, also anxious and expectant, hauled the materials free of charge, and donated some cash. The ore needful for the experiments was given by the Eureka Company, together with the use of the furnace property.

The experiments were accompanied by repeated disappointments, and many began to share the view of the leading iron experts of the North that Alabama ore was not suited to iron making. But Colonel J. W. Sloss, who directed the operations, was undismayed. He continued, through various experts, to try new methods, and finally, after months of labor, the crucial test came on June 28, 1876. On this date it was demonstrated beyond peradventure that coke iron could be produced in Birmingham.

The success of the efforts put forth by the Experimental Company had an electrical effect upon the district and marked the real beginning of the industrial expansion which led up to the great boom of the middle eighties. Furnace construction began almost immediately, hundreds of coke ovens were built, projected railroads were pushed forward, new mines were opened, and manufacturing and mercantile enterprises developed with astonishing rapidity.

Lots which had gone begging during the dark days of 1873-75 arose to dizzy heights. The stock of the Elyton Land Company, which had dropped to seventeen cents a share, went up like a skyrocket, and in 1886 every dollar originally put into it was worth $35. The dividend payments for that year amounted to 340 per cent.

The growth of Birmingham and the rapid increase in values during the ten years intervening between 1876 and 1886 attracted international attention, and brought thousands of people to the community, many of them coming with a view of making permanent investments, but others having no other idea than to make a quick turn-over and then go on their way. The latter element injected into the community the virus of inordinate speculation, and the result was an orgy of buying and selling, accompanied by the most sensational rises in value. As prices leaped skyward, and profits were pyramided, frenzy grew, and presently Birmingham was in the midst of a real estate boom that fairly appalled the conservative element.

Every train swelled the throngs of frenzied buyers until it became impossible to house the multitudes. Men bought property they had never seen and turned it over at a profit to others who were equally oblivious as to what they were buying. Lots changed hands several times in a single day while the frenzy lasted, and every transfer was at a substantial advance.

During the rush attending this orgy of speculation, it was not unnatural that even the lowly colored boy should seek to get a part of the golden fleece, and he adopted unique methods, one of which was to get in the long line that formed daily at the general delivery window of the postoffice, and, when he succeeded in drawing close to the window, sell his place to some hurried individual who wanted to lose as little time as possible in receiving his mail and getting back into the great game of profit-grabbing.

This boom illustrated once more the age-old

truth that air-castles will not stay put, and when the inevitable happened the last state of Birmingham was almost as bad as the first. About the only difference between the blow caused by the boom and that which had been caused by the cholera was that the boom hit more people and the doleful news of the collapse was carried farther.

Recovery from the baleful effects of this boom was slow and labored, and it was almost a decade before the city finally caught the pace that carried it to the present position of eminence.

During this period of sharp reaction the truth became obvious that unless domestic iron could be converted into steel upon a commercial basis, then Birmingham was destined to remain a raw material town, with cheap labor, a crude output, and a circumscribed growth.

Several attempts had been made to produce steel, but the processes proved so costly that the enterprise had to be abandoned. Events rocked along thus until 1895, when another epoch-making experiment was made at a little furnace which had been erected for the purpose, at the old rolling mill which once stood near the present Alice furnace. This experiment was approached with much the same feeling that attended the more ancient experiment of producing coke iron. Every one acquainted with the industrial life of the community felt that the production of steel upon a basis that would enable Birmingham to compete with other steel-producing centers would mean a tremendous forward step, and the result was awaited with breathless interest. Failure meant continued stagnation; success meant a new and dazzling era of expansion!

And it was success!

The steel that streamed from the white-hot mouth of that little experimental furnace proved an omen of rare good fortune. It was prophetic of the time when gigantic industries would stretch their lurid length for miles along the valley; when the products of the Birmingham district would go to the far places of the earth, and when the struggling and oft-defeated little city would take its place as one of the great industrial centers of the world!

CHAPTER VI

ROY COHEN'S NEGRO QUARTER

BIRMINGHAM'S negro quarter, made famous by Octavus Roy Cohen in his inimitable sketches, is but two blocks removed from the main artery of commerce. Twentieth Street is the Broadway of Birmingham, and most of the picture shows, soft drink emporiums and professional offices described by Cohen are two blocks west on Eighteenth Street. And a right brave showing the colored population makes upon this thoroughfare.

At night when Florian Slappey, Lawyer Chew, and thousands of their kind are abroad, the picture theatres present fronts just as dazzling as the theatres around the corner that cater to the whites, and the show windows shine with the same refulgence. Here are drug stores, haberdasheries, tailor shops, furniture stores, and kindred enterprises, and many of them wear an air of smartness creditable to both the taste and the enterprise of the proprietors.

Most of the buildings in this quarter are two-story bricks, but there is one office building six stories in height that would be a credit to any part of the city. It belongs to the colored Knights of Pythias of the State, and it is kept in beautiful condition. Housed within its walls are most of the professional men of this race, doctors, dentists, and lawyers.

Booker Washington, who founded Tuskegee Institute, was a frequent visitor to Birmingham and his influence upon the colored population was marked. His memory is revered today, and his influence for good survives. Local leaders with like ideals have been numerous, too, and the pleasant relationship which has always existed between the races in Birmingham is due largely to these influences. There has never been a race riot in this city, despite the presence of more than seventy thousand negroes, and there is not the slightest evidence of race antagonism. The Birmingham negro, guided by wise leaders, has found his groove and quietly moves within it.

The memory of Booker Washington is perpetuated in Birmingham by the Booker T. Washington

Public Library, equipped with funds raised through the colored schools of the city, but maintained by the municipality under the Public Library Board. It is a popular institution and plays an important part in the life of the colored population.

Negro churches are numerous and a number of them are huge and imposing. It was in one of these, the Shiloh Baptist, that the greatest calamity in the history of the city occurred in 1902. Booker Washington, whose appearance on the platform in this city was ever a signal for a vast outpouring, was the speaker on that occasion, and the church was packed to the doors. During the exercises some confusion arose and an excitable person cried "fight." The audience understood this cry to be "fire," and out of so small a thing arose a ghastly tragedy. There was an instant rush for the main exit, and there, in a hollow square, into which stairways from the galleries emptied, struggling humanity was piled eight to ten feet high. More than a hundred negroes were either crushed to death or smothered in this pit.

This appalling tragedy was a tremendous shock to Booker Washington, and those who were close to him feel that it did much to bring on the condition which culminated in his death a few years later.

The number of illiterates among Birmingham negroes is comparatively small, and the percentage is decreasing rapidly. Total illiteracy among blacks as a whole is eighteen and four-tenths per cent. Illiteracy exists chiefly among the older members of the race, as is illustrated by the fact that only three and eight-tenths per cent of illiterates are found among members of the race between sixteen and twenty years of age.

This steady decrease in illiteracy is due to the excellent school facilities provided in Birmingham for the colored population, and to the strong emphasis placed upon education by negro leaders. Compulsory education, a new thing in Alabama, will bring about a more rapid advance in future years.

The Industrial High School for Negroes, a part of the public school system of Birmingham, is doing really a wonderful work in training the colored youth for a life of usefulness. Manual training is stressed strongly, and the students have the opportunity to learn many useful occupations. Shoemaking, tailoring, carpentry, auto-mechanics, printing and similar trades are taught, while girls have domestic science, dressmaking and nursing, Members of the nursing class proved a veritable boon to the city during the epidemic of influenza which swept the country in 1919. Here, as elsewhere, the number of professional nurses was wholly inadequate to meet the situation, and the presence of scores of well-trained high school students, who were willing to assist in the emergency, proved a real blessing to the community.

While, as indicated in the foregoing, illiteracy is fast disappearing among the negroes, there remains a sufficient number of the old-time darkies, with their ignorance and superstition, to furnish endless amusement to the observant.

For a number of years my work as a newspaper reporter carried me to jails, morgues and courts, places where the tragic note dominates nine-tenths of the time, and where the darky always is in evidence. Recalling these scenes now, I seem to review a long procession of dead bodies and dead hopes, yet amid these sombre surroundings occurred some of the most amusing things that ever came under my observation, the central figure being usually a negro.

One of the morgues I visited daily was where many of the victims of railroad and mining accidents were sent to be prepared for burial, and it was a dull day when some still form was not stretched out upon one of the long marble slabs. In addition to the reporters, whose duty required them to visit this place daily, there was an aged darky who came practically every day, curiosity being the sole incentive. His manner of approach was the same always. Reaching the front door, he would take off his hat in a reverential manner and step softly into the office; then approaching the manager in the most insinuating manner, he would ask: "Boss, is you got any corpses today?" Whenever the reply was in the affirmative, he would ask: "Can I view the 'mains?"

On such occasions, if there happened to be in the house the body of a negro man, the manager would say, "Come on," and would lead the old darky back into the gloomy hall, where were the marble slabs and the motionless figures.

Entering the room with obvious terror, yet drawn by some irresistible fascination, the negro would watch as the sheet was drawn back and gaze awe-stricken upon the cold, expressionless face of the dead. Then he would utter a sigh and take his departure.

This happened time and time again, and finally the old man became an institution. If the afternoon papers chronicled a wreck or an explosion, and told of the victims having been carried to this establishment, "Old Curiosity," as he had become known, was always on hand the following morning, eager to view the "'mains."

For months this darky enjoyed the intoxication of terror, but all things have an end, as one learns by contact with a morgue, and the visits of "Old Curiosity" terminated finally, the end coming in this fashion:

One dull summer day several of the boys were chatting in the front office, when the approach of the darky was observed. The manager was out at the time, and one of his assistants, whose bump of humor had flourished prodigiously even among unfavorable surroundings, said, "Send him back, boys; I am going to get under a sheet on Slab One," and he fled to the morgue.

"Boss, has you got any corpses today?" the old man asked as he entered the door.

"Yes," replied one of the reporters, "just go back and look under the sheet on Slab One."

Thus enjoined, the darky edged his way into the gloomy back room, and, stopping at Slab One, gingerly drew down the sheet. As he did so the "corpse" looked him straight in the eye and inquired:

"What the deuce do you want, nigger?"

With a yell of terror, the darky dropped the sheet and fled from the place, moving with a speed that was highly complimentary to his aged legs. So far as I know, he never returned. The cure was complete.

The attitude of "Old Curiosity" is typical of the ignorant among the blacks. They dearly love a funeral, and a cadaver has for them a mighty fascination, yet they are terrified beyond measure at anything suggestive of the supernatural.

At another undertaking establishment on my "beat" two negroes were called on to bring a basket down stairs from an upper room. They learned too late that the basket, which was covered with a sheet, contained the body of a man who had died only a short time before, and they were in a rather nervous state when they started down the stairs, one at either end of the basket. They had taken only a few steps downward when the corpse was seen deliberately to draw up its knees. As the knees came up the negroes loosed their hold, and, with cries of terror, tumbled pell-mell down the stairway, followed by the basket, the body and the winding sheet. The corpse finally came to a stop, as did the basket and the sheet, but not so the negroes. They kept going, and from that time on they cut this establishment from their calling list.

What had happened was this: The negroes, in going down the stairs, had allowed the foot of the basket to drop so low that the body, which had not become rigid, slipped downward, forcing the knees to come up exactly as if the corpse had moved of its own volition. The thing was so life-like that one could not blame the negroes for assuming that the dead was manifesting unorthodox activity.

A little comedy, the final act of which I witnessed in the police court, started directly in front of this undertaking establishment. A well known and eminently respectable citizen was walking by the place when, without warning, he was seized by a husky young negro, who not only embraced him in a most enthusiastic manner, but seemed disposed to do a cake-walk with him there upon the public street. The two struggled violently for a brief period and then a policeman rushed up and pried them apart.

The negro was carried to jail, and on the following morning, when the case was called, the gentleman who had been assaulted took the stand and swore that he was walking along quietly, when, without the slightest provocation, the defendant leaped upon him and attempted to throw him. He had never seen the negro before, so far as he knew, and could offer no explanation of the act. Several other witnesses were called, their testimony being along the same lines.

The negro, a quiet and docile creature, as he appeared in the court room, had no witnesses, but was represented by a police court lawyer, who was recognized as an unusually resourceful young man. The lawyer paid little attention to the evidence,

THE SKY-LINE, RED MOUNTAIN IN THE BACKGROUND

except to develop the fact that there existed no known cause for malice. When the evidence was in, he addressed the court as follows:

"If your honor please, no evidence has been produced here to show premeditation. On the other hand, all that has been said tends to prove the act of my client to have been involuntary, and this, if it please the court, is the truth, as I shall show you.

"My client, if it please the court, is what is known as a 'goosy' negro ——"

"A what?" exclaimed the court.

"A 'goosy' negro, if it please your honor; that is to say, he is so constituted that if any one pokes a finger against his person he involuntarily throws his arms about any object that happens to be in front of him. He can't help it, your honor, and this is what happened; the defendant was 'goosed' by some one at the moment the gentleman was passing, and, obeying this uncontrollable impulse, he threw his arms about the first object at hand, which happened to be the complainant."

The judge reached for his pen and was about to write "ten dollars and costs" across the docket, intending afterward to compliment the lawyer upon the ingenuity of his defense, when the arresting officer conceived the idea of giving a demonstration of the absurdity of the lawyer's contention. With this end in view, he poked an experimental finger into the ribs of the darky.

When this happened the accused was standing at the bar, directly in front of his lawyer. As the stubby finger of the officer came in contact with his person he uttered a startled cry and, at the same moment, threw his arms about the lawyer and began to do a war-dance, the genuine nature of which no witness could question. The spectators howled their delight as three brawny blue-coats applied themselves to the task of rescuing the badly tousled disciple of Blackstone.

When the judge succeeded in getting the water out of his eyes — water being one of the by-products of laughter — he inscribed "not guilty" opposite the name of the darky and called the next case.

It was in this court that I witnessed the acquittal of a negro woman who won her freedom by reducing the prosecuting witness to a state of coma with a blow upon the head — a rather unusual method of obtaining a verdict, even in a police court.

The defendant in this case was an old colored "mammy" who weighed about ninety pounds and had a face as black as the inside of a powder can. The prosecuting witness was a yellow negress about twenty years of age, and as flip of lip as women of her type get to be. She had caused the arrest of the old woman on a charge of using profane and abusive language. She took the stand and began a dramatic recital of what the defendant was alleged to have said, and the language she attributed to that old "mammy" was as lurid as ever fell from vulgar lips.

As the vile recital went forward the small black eyes of the old woman darted lightning and her body was as tense as a steel spring. Suddenly she leaped to her feet, seized a chair, whirled it above her head and brought it down with a resounding crash upon the head of that glib young thing. "You brazen huzzy," she screamed, "you can't lie about me like that."

Officers seized her, while other court attendants picked up the form of the yellow girl, which had crumpled to the floor. Meanwhile the judge, wise of the ways of colored folk, inscribed "Not guilty" after the name of the black "mammy."

The guileless character of the average negro is an asset in his favor when he is brought into court, since the Southern judge has an uncanny gift of reading what is going on under the woolly crown, but this characteristic develops some odd situations at times, as is illustrated by the experience of a lawyer when called upon to handle the case of a negro who was charged with the theft of a cow. The lawyer had known the negro for a long time, and, believing him to be thoroughly honest, he agreed to take a note for the fee, which amounted to $50.

In due time the case was tried, and under the skillful handling of the lawyer a verdict of acquittal was obtained. Shortly thereafter the darky called at the office of the attorney and paid the note in full.

"It's rather tough on you to have to pay out so much money after all the trouble you had over this case," observed the lawyer.

"Oh, it ain't as bad as it might be," replied the darkey, "I got $35 for the cow and only had to put up $15 myself."

The same lawyer was knocked breathless by the conduct of another guileless member of the colored race in the trial of a case in which the accused was under indictment for an alleged wrong against a negro woman.

In the preparation of the defense it developed that the woman making the charge was a most notorious character, and while the defendant admitted being the recipient of some of her favors, it was clear that he was one among many. Under the circumstances the lawyer advised the accused to tell the court and the jury the whole truth, assuring him that the evidence against the woman's character would result in his acquittal. To this plan the negro agreed fully and without hesitation.

When the case came to trial, the character of the woman was blackened beyond redemption, and it remained only for the accused to speak his little piece and receive his discharge.

"The defendant will take the stand," announced the lawyer, and the darky stepped into the witness box, from which point of vantage his eyes roamed over the audience.

"Now," enjoined the lawyer, "tell the jury about your relations with this woman."

"She ain't no relation o' mine," replied the witness. "What's more, I never seen her in my life 'til I cum into this here court, an' I ain't never had nuthin a-tall to do with her. It's just a plum pack o' lies, and besides I's got too good a wife to home to be trapsin' aroun' with no other woman."

As the defendant reeled off this astonishing fabrication the jaw of his lawyer sagged, and he looked at the witness for a moment as if stupefied. Then he gasped. "That's all; the defense closes."

At the first opportunity the lawyer asked his client, "Why in the world did you get up there and tell what everybody in this court room knows to be a lie, when I instructed you to tell the truth?"

"Well, Boss," replied the darky, in apologetic tones, "I guess you don't know my wife is here among them present, else you wouldn't expect me to make no such 'knowledgments. I didn't know she was anywhere abouts 'til I got on the stand an' saw her sittin' back there with a hickory stick in her han's, then I made up my min' sudden like that it'd be a whole lot better to take chances on gettin' convicted here than to get my head peeled with that stick when I gets outside."

The defendant was acquitted, and, fortunately for him, he did not have to face a trial for perjury.

The colored widow who went into a store and, after buying a black dress, asked to be shown some black underwear, saying, "When I mourns, I mourns," illustrated a familiar attribute of the darky. When he lies, he lies with utter abandon, and when he determines to stick to the truth, he does it with admirable tenacity, which reminds me of another court scene, one that I did not have the pleasure of witnessing, but which was described to me as authentic.

The case in which this incident developed involved the title to a valuable plantation, and one of the most important witnesses was a colored farmer. Recognizing the vital nature of the negro's evidence, the gentleman whose property was in litigation did all he could to impress upon the witness the importance of understanding fully every question asked him during the trial of the case. "You will be asked a great many questions," he said, "and the lawyers on the other side will do all they can to confuse you. So take plenty of time and be sure you know what the question is before you make any attempt to answer." Thus schooled, the negro took the stand when the case was called, and thereupon the following dialogue occurred:

"What's your name?" asked the lawyer.

"Fust name or last name?" countered the witness.

"Both."

"My fust name is Bill for short an' my last name is Johnson."

"Well, Bill, where do you live?"

"Whatcher mean, town or county?"

"I mean town and county."

"I don't live in no town."

"Then where do you live?"

"I lives on the Warrior River near Car-dovy."

"Which side of the river do you live on?"

"Whatcher mean, goin' up 'er or down 'er?"

"Well, suppose we say going up her?"

"Goin' up 'er I lives on the right side; goin' down 'er I lives on the left side."

"Can you read?"

"Whatcher mean, printin' or writin'?"

"Can you read either printing or writing?"

"No, suh."

"Say," exclaimed the lawyer, who had become somewhat irritated by the subdued giggles his encounter with the darky had evoked, "ar'n't you something of a fool?"

"Whatcher mean, a plain 'un or a dam 'un?" asked the negro, and the court found it necessary to call on the bailiff to restore order.

However, not all negroes are such sticklers for accuracy. I recall visiting a negro in his cell one morning just before he was to be led forth to the gallows. Face to face with the unfathomable things of eternity, this darky had groped about for some limb of truth upon which he might hang his faith, and this is what he had found: "Blessed is them that is persecuted." With this phrase fixed firmly in his mind, he paced his narrow cell, repeating the words over and over, "The good Lord says, 'Blessed is them that is persecuted.'" And thus he went to his death, a poor trembling wretch, knowing not that he had left off the clause "for righteousness sake" in quoting the promise of the Savior, and ignorant also of the distinction between the words "persecuted" and "prosecuted."

The story is told that a condemned negro, when standing upon the gallows, was asked if he had any statement to make before the end, and that he replied:

"All I got to say is that this sure is goin' to be a powerful lesson to me."

So it must have been with reference to the executions they had with such frequency in those long-gone days when, in the capacity of a reporter, I stood in the high-walled yard back of that old jail and saw so many criminals drop through the trap to be brought up short at the end of a taut and merciless rope. Those grim illustrations of the power and the purpose of outraged law must have made a profound impression upon the race, both black and white, for hangings have become less frequent, although Birmingham's population has increased five-fold since that period, and there has been a steady growth in the demand for law enforcement.

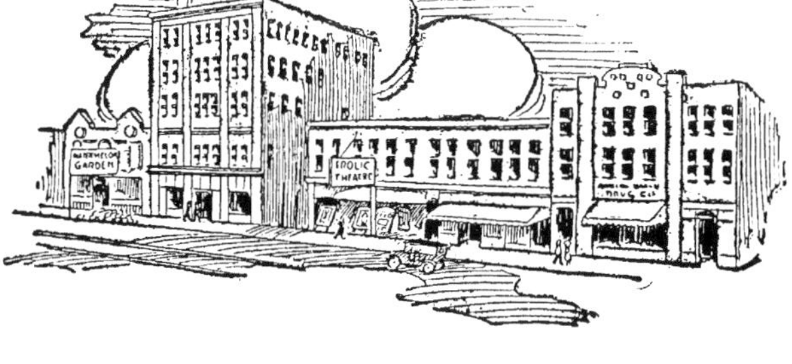

CHAPTER VII

VISIONS OF BEAUTY

THE Bee Line Highway, over which thousands of tourists flock back and forth with the changing seasons, enters from the South at a long bridge spanning the Cahaba River. When the automobile rolls across this bridge into Jefferson County, of which Birmingham is the center, it is upon a magnificent road, perfect in construction and exceptional in scenic beauty. There begins at once a slow but steady climb toward the peak of Shades Mountain, from the crest of which green valleys stretch into the distance, and to the South of which lies Red Mountain, yet to be negotiated before Birmingham is reached.

Dropping down Shades Mountain on the perfect asphalt road is an experience one cannot forget.

While the Southern slope is gentle, the fall to the North is abrupt, and the highway zig-zags in a most astonishing manner. The roadway is laid upon a series of shelves, cut into the mountain side, and as the terminus of each shelf is reached there is a sharp reverse curve, leading to the next. On one hand the mountain rises sheer, while on the other it drops at times to fearsome depths. Fences, beautifully white, or, at more dangerous points, strong stone walls, warn the tourist of the danger, and accidents are few. But always there is the exhilaration that comes with a suggestion of peril.

Another bridge and another river, and when one crosses there begins the ascent of Red Mountain, out of whose heart comes much of the iron that feeds the furnaces of this district. As in the case of Shades Mountain, the ascent here is somewhat gradual, while the Northern slope is even more abrupt than that of Shades Mountain.

Let us hope that the tourist who comes over this highway reaches the peak of Red Mountain just as the shades of night have fallen, for it is then that the scene becomes most entrancing.

As the peak of the mountain is approached, the road drops into a deep cut, spanned at the very top by a railroad bridge. As the car rolls from under this bridge, upon the high Northern shelf of the mountain, there bursts upon the vision — Birmingham. Not a glimpse of the city until now, and now a glorious vision of the whole!

Three hundred feet below it stretches mile on mile. A million stars seem to sparkle down there in the purple darkness, while to the right and to the left, and in the far, vague background, there glows the deep red of furnace fires; fires that turn the evening heavens into rose and lend fantastic beauty to the fleecy clouds. Lights glow in forty thousand homes. Row upon row, the street lamps stretch into the distance, and just below, in the very heart of the city, huge office buildings tower high, their forms but vaguely sketched in dreamy squares of light. To the right, far below, two arcs of radiance are clearly seen, marking the curvature of the magnificent new viaduct which spans the railroads and carries one into the very heart of the city.

How many times have I come through that gap in Red Mountain, with vision circumscribed by towering banks of red, and then paused at the exit to gaze entranced upon the picture below! Beautiful Birmingham, beautiful in its setting, beautiful in the character and the ideals of its people, and beautiful in the nature of its accomplishments! One cannot gaze upon you here without feeling the presence of something fine and sweet and true.

Your starry reaches suggest the infinite; your night-time beauty the City Celestial!

Dropping down Red Mountain, one is in the city at once, Birmingham's most fashionable residential district hugging the side of these heights for several miles. One may turn sharply to the left after descending the mountain for a half mile, and be in the center of the business district in five minutes, or he can go mile on mile along beautiful highways that twist and bend and rise and fall as they lend themselves to the changing contour. From Highland Avenue, the beauty of which is known the country over, he sweeps up the mountain through Milner Heights, and there, after performing a wide circuit that affords a fine view of the sleeping valley to the South, he comes again to the Northern crest of the mountain, and again beholds the panorama of Birmingham from a roadway that seems ever ready to tumble into the depths below, restrained only by a stout stone wall that parallels its Northern side.

To the North there is a sharp descent, and then another swift climb along a circuitous route, which leads again to Milner Crescent, and back to Highland Avenue. Along this thoroughfare for a mile, and there is Cliff Road. It becomes steep at once, but the car can negotiate the grade, straight-away. In a little while, however, there comes a sharp reverse curve, and then back and forth, tier upon tier, the road zig-zags up the mountain. There another circuit to the right, and then back to the same point, from whence, straight ahead, are twin-highways, one running up to the very peak of a higher point on the mountain, and the other trailing along a lower shelf. These highways unite beyond this peak, and then comes another sharp descent, this time through Mountain Terrace, and back again to Highland Avenue.

Reaching Lower Highland Avenue, one is again confronted with a choice of parallel routes, one sweeping by the lake that nestles in front of the Country Club, and the other along the Eastern crest of Chestnut Hill. Three great stone stairways connect these parallel highways between the points of divergence, adding to the dignity and charm of the scene.

From here the tourist might turn again toward the mountain and run over asphalt roads to two beautiful and highly exclusive residential parks, Glen Iris and Idlewild, but it is time to see something of the hills beyond the city, so he continues along Lower Highland Avenue to Twenty-First Street, across the long and graceful viaduct which spans the railroads, and so through the business section to the North Highlands. Here the ground rises almost as high as it does on the South side, but the ascent is so gradual that one scarcely is conscious of the change in altitude.

To the East is Norwood, the central feature of which is the winding boulevard two hundred feet in width, with a parkway running through its center from end to end. Here, on summer days, honeysuckles bloom in wild profusion, and the night air is sweet with their subtle odor. All along the way Crepe-myrtle bushes almost attain the dignity of trees, and there are thousands of climbing roses, calla-lilies and other blossoms to greet the eye when such things are in season.

Homes, ranging from dainty bungalows to palatial mansions, flank all these splendid driveways, the largest and most costly being found in the South Highlands section. Noting the wild topography in some quarters, one is disposed to wonder at the courage of the men who dared to convert such rugged hillsides into the dwelling places. On many winding thoroughfares the ground rises sharply on one hand and falls with equal sharpness on the other, the homes upon one side standing high above the roadway, upon such steep inclines that one marvels they do not slip from their foundations; while on the other the houses are on a level with the street in front, but have in some cases two and even three floors below the level in the rear.

How to beautify homes so situated must have been a puzzling problem in the beginning, but this, like many other problems connected with the building of the city, was solved in a happy fashion, and the surroundings of many of these queerly placed residences are striking in their originality. Multiple terraces in the front, and sunken gardens, dropping one below the other, at the rear, form a common scheme of landscape architecture.

The hero of many of these amazing ventures upon rugged mountain sides, where frowning walls have been converted into places of beauty and utility, is "Young Bob" Jemison, called "Young," to distinguish him from his father, Robert, Sr., who also belonged to the pioneer class, having been one of the prime movers in establishing mail routes in Alabama before the coming of the railroad, and later, doing a man's size job in developing a street railway system in Birmingham. In those old stage-coach days, Robert Jemison, Sr., resided at Tuscaloosa, the ancient capital of Alabama, and Colonel James R. Powell, then of Montgomery, but who afterwards became the "Duke of Birmingham," were rivals in this line. They were close competitors for the postal business of the government, and their fight for passenger traffic was equally warm. Each was forced to recognize the mettle of the other, and in the end they consoli-

A VISTA FROM RED MOUNTAIN

dated their interest, and became giants in the stage-coach game, holding their own against all rivals until the coming of the railroads.

When "Young Bob," full of the fighting spirit of his sire, undertook to cut highways along the forbidding side of Red Mountain, many thought he would be sent back to the ancestral home in Tuscaloosa, where is located the institution for the repair of broken-down mental machinery, since there seemed no place upon which to put houses along some of these highways. But that was long ago, and now the highways are flanked by beautiful homes and "Young Bob" is conceded to have sense as well as sand.

Another bold explorer of land that lies mostly on edge is "Key" Milner, son of Major W. J. Milner, who was one of the founders of Birmingham and who not only designed that wonderful thoroughfare, Highland Avenue, but built the great water works system which today supplies the city, and also was a pioneer in the transportation field. It was in mapping a route for a "dummy line" that Major Milner designed Highland Avenue. By a "dummy line" is meant a street railway on which cars are drawn by a steam engine, snugly ensconced in what looks like a cross between a modern street car and an ancient tool house. To his son is due the development of one of Birmingham's most beautiful mountain-side residential districts. It has been said that only three animals would have invaded the mountain sides as they have been invaded here, the three being "Young Bob," "Key," and the mountain goat.

Since the mountain sides were conquered some years ago, the time of home building has swept to the crest, and today many splendid residences stand on the very top. Indeed, the most palatial homes in the city are found upon these heights; the cost running from tens of thousands to hundreds of thousands. This is a new development, however, and wide spaces separate the homes at this time.

In addition to the heights described above, there is a third great division known as the Ensley Highlands, situated in the Western portion of the city and overlooking the vast industrial section that stretches on toward the setting sun. The ground here is not so high and rugged as on Red Mountain, but it has been beautifully improved and contains many handsome homes. This section was developed largely through the vision of R. A. Terrell, another conspicuous figure among the farseeing pioneers.

In the long and winding valley between these heights are a dozen or more residence communities where live the thousands whose bank rolls are not plethoric. Snug bungalows predominate in most of these communities, but in practically all of them there are a number of large and pretentious homes.

Particularly is this true of Elyton, the ancient county site, long since swallowed up by the city which took away its court house in that amazing election in 1872. Here, upon a beautiful knoll, with wide stretches of green, stands the old colonial residence of R. S. Munger, millionaire inventor of the Munger gin, while all around are clustered handsome homes of the most modern type.

While several suburban communities have grown up hap-hazard, having failed to learn the lesson in city planning from Birmingham, a number of these centers of population were developed with the aid of skilled landscape architects, and have about them none of the ear-marks of accidental growth.

Fairfield, one of the larger suburbs, where many employees of the Steel Corporation subsidiaries reside, has been given unstinted praise by Colonel Roosevelt, by Maude Adams, and by others interested in making proper provision for the toiler. A splendid boulevard, with a parkway running through its center, constitutes the main thoroughfare, while from it radiates numerous streets and avenues that would be a credit to any residence community.

Westleigh and Central Park were designed by the same architect, and are dotted with snug and attractive dwellings. East Lake, Woodlawn, Avondale, North Birmingham and West End are older suburbs that have grown harmoniously and possess the air of restfulness and comfort that belongs to communities peopled by home-owning and home-loving citizens.

The Tennessee Coal, Iron & Railroad Company, and other subsidiaries of the United States Steel Corporation, long ago adopted a policy of surrounding their various enterprises with a wholesome atmosphere, and throughout the entire Birmingham district may be found communities where the greatest care has been given the matter of housing. In many instances even the smallest homes have been given marks of distinction, and in numerous cases an additional incentive is given for adding charm to these small dwellings. Prizes are offered from time to time to stimulate interest in making the communities more attractive, and every effort is made to keep alive the spirit of pride in home and town. Unhappily, this spirit did not dominate in the early days, and in cousequence there are a number of communities in the mining fields where such matters have been neglected. However, the encouraging thing is that no new communities are forming without having about them some suggestion of appreciation for beauty as well as utility. "Model camps" have become the ideal in mining circles, and conditions steadily are improving. So much for the power of example.

Regardless of what has been said, or what may be said, about the absorption of the Tennessee Company by the Steel Corporation, it generally is conceded in Alabama that the development was a fortunate one. The Tennessee Company was desperately hard up most of the time and had no money for applying artistic touches. No grim struggle for existence faces the present owners, and the time and money necessary for making flowers grow about industrial plants has been forthcoming.

Another gratifying thing is the spirit of co-operation which exists between the great industrial agencies and the municipalities with which they come in contact. This attitude is illustrated by the fact that more than half the cost of Birmingham's latest, largest and most modern public swimming pool was contributed by the Tennessee Company. This great double pool, placed in Ensley Park, cost $48,000, and $25,000 of the amount was given to the city by the company because thousands of its employees reside in that community. The expenditures of this company along æsthetic lines are lavish and the results obtained in many instances are astounding.

In Acipco, another suburb, a new school was erected recently by the Board of Education of Birmingham, and the American Cast Iron Pipe Company contributed $25,000 to the cost of the structure in order that it might be equipped with reading rooms, a lecture hall, and other features for community use. The company also aided materially in fitting up the playgrounds which surround the school. This organization maintains a Young Men's Christian Association building, recreational fields, shower baths, etc., for all its employees. Its homes for negro workers are models of utility, each one being provided with a bathroom — a new and extraordinary departure.

The Stockham Pipe & Fittings Company, another large industrial agency, provides a Y. M. C. A. building with numerous attractive features, and makes every effort to combine wholesome and happy living with utilitarianism.

The Republic Iron & Steel Company, which recently tendered a large piece of property to the city for school purposes, has surrounded its works at Thomas with numerous evidences of appreciation for the beautiful. The Sloss, the Woodward and other companies also count money spent in this fashion as money well invested, and the result here has been to close forever that unhappy period when the building of mills and the opening of mines meant the establishment of towns characterized by stark and naked ugliness.

CHAPTER VIII

THE PEOPLE AT PLAY

IN the very beginning the founders of Birmingham, composed largely of young men, recognized the necessity of recreational features, and in the original plans provisions was made for a number of parks, the property being dedicated for this purpose. Among the earliest structures was a pavilion for recreational purposes, and here the people met to dance, to enjoy an occasional concert of amateur entertainment, or to hear the issues of the day discussed by the orators of that period. In naming this pavilion, the sense of humor, so pronounced in those first days, was again in evidence. It was "The Crystal Palace," 'though hastily thrown together and made of rough lumber, and having no crystal about it unless an occasional pitcher on the speaker's stand could be counted under this heading.

Today, after the passage of fifty years, Birmingham still is a young man's town. Its growth during the past twenty years has exceeded a hundred and fifty thousand, and a large part of this increase is accounted for by the fact that young men have been attracted here in large numbers because of the opportunities created by the rapidly expanding industrial and commercial life. This condition has brought about a constantly growing demand for recreational features, and sports thrive here to an unusual extent.

The topography of the land, not unlike a storm-tossed ocean, is peculiarly adapted for golf, and two splendid country clubs have links that are a source of delight to devotees of this sport.

The Country Club, the oldest and most popular organization, has extensive grounds well within the city limits and within a few minutes' ride of the heart of the city. The club house, a beautiful and spacious building, nestles upon a shelf of Red Mountain, while in the foreground is a charming lake. To the right of this lake the links roll off into the distance, presenting an entrancing view and offering rare sport to followers of the pitted ball.

The Roebuck Springs Golf Club lies up the valley nine miles from the heart of the city, being reached by a paved thoroughfare. It, too, has an attractive club house with a sparkling lake in front, and is surrounded by grounds of great natural charm. The links rank among the best in the South and are the scene of many spirited contests.

Baseball, the great national sport, has the community firmly in its grasp, and this city usually leads the Southern League in point of attendance. Rickwood Field, where the games are staged, is not only one of the most modern baseball plants in the country, but is a perpetual advertisement of Birmingham's resources. Go to a game and open a conversation with your neighbor. If he is a Birmingham man, and he learns that you are a stranger, he will unfold a story that will run about like this:

"See that mountain over there?"

Superfluous question, for the mountain looms before you, dark and green, except where it has been torn asunder and forced to disgorge its metallic content, but you answer "Yes."

"Well," he will proceed, "the iron that entered into this steel structure was dug from that mountain. When you leave the stand after the game, look over to the West and you will see smoke arising from the furnace where the ore was smelted, and just beyond that point you will notice a series of towering stacks. That's where the iron was converted into steel. Beyond that point is the mill where the steel was fabricated into girders, just as you see them here. Not only so, but within a few miles of this very spot is the mine from which the coal was dug that furnished the fuel for transforming the ore into iron and the iron into steel. And that's not all the story: You will note that the grandstand and bleachers are made of concrete. Well, if your eyes could pierce that mountain over there you would be able to see the smudge of smoke above one of the greatest cement manufacturing plants in the South. In other words, all the materials entering into this huge plant were produced within a few miles of where we are sitting. Can you beat it?"

You acknowledge that you can't and the local citizen smiles his approval.

Coveleskie, one of the world's great pitchers, once belonged to the Birmingham team, and established here the record that carried him into the big league and thence to fame. This, however. was not the Coveleskie who, while pitching for Philadelphia, once overlooked the fact that there was a man on first and allowed the runner to go to second, and who thereby became the butt of a caustic joke by Manager Murray. "Honestly," Coveleskie explained to Murray on leaving the box, "I didn't know that there was a man on first." "Oh, you didn't," purred Murray, "then, of course, that makes it all right." He then called Eddie Grant over and said to him: "The next time there is a man on first, I want you to go over and tell Covie all about it. I'm not going to have any secrets among my players."

The hero of this incident was a brother of the Birmingham Coveleskie.

Frank Smith, who also became a top-notcher when promoted to the big league, was a Birmingham player, and he carried with him the fame of having knocked the longest drive ever seen on the local diamond. It cleared the left field bases — and the bases.

While Smith was cleaning up all the rival Southern League teams with his swift and puzzling curves, and was at the height of his Southern League fame, he suddenly disappeared on one occasion and was not seen for several days. Shortly after his return from this mysterious absence, the story leaked out that he had been over to a small town in Georgia where the local fans had made up their minds to beat a rival team if it took all the money in the town. With this end in view, they made a secret deal with the South's premier pitcher. The result was an overwhelming victory — not for them but for the hated rivals. Those town-lot boys from the neighboring village pounded the "premier" to a fare-you-well, and walked off with the game. So far as I know, they are still ignorant of the identity of the great pitcher they lambasted on that occasion.

Birmingham has two attractive amusement parks, East Lake, owned and operated by the city, and Edgewood Park, privately owned. Recreational parks are numerous but are not well developed. Two of these parks, one containing a hundred acres and the other two hundred acres, are endowed with great natural beauty, but as yet have not been developed by the municipality. But while the city lags in the improvement of its larger parks, great progress has been made in the matter of playgrounds. These playgrounds are numerous, well equipped and are given competent supervision. Moreover, the number is multiplying with great rapidity, showing an evident determination to provide properly for the young life of the community. During the present year two public swimming pools were opened, one representing an investment of nearly $50,000 and being perfect in its appointments, including a violet ray purification plant.

Where the city is notably lax is in its failure to provide parks for the colored population. This is due, as is the failure properly to improve the large undeveloped parks set aside for white people, to the fact that for years the city operated upon inadequate revenues. Until 1920, when a constitutional amendment was adopted granting an increase of fifty cents in the tax rate, Birmingham's rate was one dollar on the one hundred dollars — the lowest of any city in its class in the United States. Under the circumstances the municipality was able to provide little beyond the bare necessities. However, with a fifty per cent increase in the tax income, effective in 1921, it is probable that substantial progress will be made along the lines of park development. The program of improvement includes at least one park exclusively for the colored population.

The Warrior River, which furnishes Birmingham with water transportation to the Gulf, is growing as a recreational center for the citizens of Birmingham who own automobiles, and it holds forth promise of becoming a great factor in the life of the community with the development of transportation facilities.

The Warrior constitutes the greatest canalized stream in America, and with the erection of the mighty dams which made it navigable to Birminghamport, vast areas were inundated between the mountains that stretch for miles along the course of the stream, and more picturesque scenes scarcely could be imagined. Some of these mountains are covered thickly with towering trees, green as em-

WHERE CHILDREN MAKE MERRY—CITY PARK

erald in summer and shot with radiance in the early winter, while others display immense outcroppings of limestone. Frequently one may see, imbedded in this soft and porous stone, great spheres of harder stone, as though some giant had moulded cannon balls of molten granite and shot them into the softer stone. The water, which backs into every valley, is beautifully clear, and contains bass, perch, brim, and other varieties of fish. Numerous rough camps, open to vacationists, have been established along the river and its tributaries, but no comprehensive scheme of developing the wonderful recreational possibilities has been adopted as yet. That this will come in the future is certain. Meanwhile almost perfect highways furnish a ready means of reaching the scene, and thousands go there during the summer months.

For those who want their recreation at their elbow, so to speak, Birmingham provides two splendid institutions in the Young Men's Christian Association and the Birmingham Athletic Club. These buildings stand cheek-by-jowl on Twentieth Street, within a few minutes' walk of the center of town, and, forming the third in a wholesome trinity, is the Southern Club. These three buildings, all in a row, seem to typify the get-together spirit of the community in which they function. The Southern Club is the pioneer social club of the city and occupies a pre-eminent position. Its home is commodious, dignified and restful. The Y. M. C. A. is much the larger building of the three and houses a virile organization which is playing a tremendous part in the lives of the young men of the community. Sandwiched between the two, the Athletic Club maintains a remarkably active organization, staging many thrilling ring events and furnishing worthy competitors in athletic contests throughout the South. The Phoenix Club, a fashionable Jewish organization, has both a handsome City Club on the South Highlands, and a Country Club on Shades Mountain.

If eating may be classed as a form of recreation, then Birmingham has an unlimited number of clubs with recreational features, in addition to those above referred to. Here the luncheon club flourishes with an abandon equal to that of the palm upon a tropical isle. Where two or three kindred spirits are gathered together, they form themselves into a luncheon club, and life becomes just one meal after another. They eat in hotels, in clubs, in ball-rooms, in billiard halls, in sample rooms, and wherever else the spreading of a table is found to be feasible.

It has been estimated that if all the plates set before Birmingham luncheon clubs within a month were placed edge to edge they would form a line extending from the foot of Red Mountain to the Gulf of Mexico, provided the waiter didn't smash too many in the process of handling. Efforts of approximate volume of oratory flowing before these clubs from week to week are recognized as futile. The usual program is thirty minutes for eating and conversation and thirty minutes for business and oratory, and it opens a fine field for the budding Demosthenese. In truth, numerous speakers have fairly eaten their way to fame by cultivating the luncheon club habit.

The humorist, too, has his day of opportunity at these clubs, and once a reputation for wit has been established, then woe to the guilty person. He has opened for himself an avenue that develops into a veritable treadmill. He is expected to make the people laugh on every occasion, so life becomes just one joke after another, without a single ray of hope. The humorist arises from his restless couch at the call of the new day, senses the sunshine and the voice of the birds, and is just about to say "What a glorious thing is life," when there rushes upon him the awful truth that at noon on that very day he must be funny — must stand before long rows of expectant faces and crack these faces into grins.

Consider the case of Frank Rushton, past president of the Rotary Club, and a quiet and unassuming business man, who was called to leadership in all the bond selling and money raising drives throughout the war. In assuming this position he inadvertently dropped a few funny remarks — and was lost. Thenceforward, with shafts of sharp and ready wit, he was expected to prick the jaded workers into newness of life at every luncheon, and long before the conflict ended he had learned the fullness of the idea General Sherman sought to convey in defining mortal conflict. So with the others who happened to strike the popular funny bone. They had to keep it up or join the ranks of the hermits. The luncheon club will have its laugh.

The popularity of these clubs is founded upon the fact that they afford the men of the community an opportunity to get together at the noon hour to discuss matters of moment, and most of them play a highly useful part in the life of the city.

It was through the agency of these clubs that prompt and glorious results were obtained during the World War whenever a subscription campaign of any kind had to be put over. During that period of exacting demands Birmingham went beyond its quota upon every bond selling campaign, and in every instance when the call for help was sent out by the great relief agencies. This really remarkable record was made possible by reason of the fact that Birmingham men had formed the habit of getting together at noontime and disposing of their problems along with their lunch.

The Rotarians, the Kiwanians, and the Civitans all have strong organizations, and their influence is attested by the fact that the international presidents of two of these clubs have been Birmingham men — Mercer Barnett, of the Kiwanians, and Dr. Courtney W. Shropshire, of the Civitans. The younger men of the city are banded together in the Community Club, and there are numerous others representing every branch of society. Even the Red Heads have their organization, and while the Bald Heads have not yet gotten together, the chances are that they will as soon as the town is a little older and their numbers have grown somewhat.

In addition to the regularly organized luncheon clubs, there are luncheon clubs within clubs that are not luncheon, if you get my meaning, and so the chefs are kept busy and the willing speaker never lacks for an audience. Vim, vigor and vitality characterize these clubs, and when they get behind anything it moves. When there is nothing important to get behind, then there is frequent horse-play and some remarkable stunts are pulled, all testifying to the existence of a spirit of exuberance that is a manifest product of youth, optimism and boundless energy.

A live and efficient organization is the Birmingham Automobile Club, which maintains headquarters in the Tutwiler, the largest hotel in the city. This club is highly useful to tourists in steering them along the right road, and in seeing that the road is in good condition. Then there is a Bicycle Club. Yes, a Bicycle Club, and every little while the members get together and are off on a long jaunt, returning weary and perspiring but happy in the knowledge that they have put one over on the gasoline man. On a recent excursion one member appeared riding a bicycle of the vintage of 1875; the kind with the huge wheel in front and the little wheel behind, and which seems ever on the verge of turning a somersault.

Horseback riding also is popular with a goodly number of men and women, especially among the younger set, 'though many of the latter show a disposition to press the toe upon an imaginary accelerator, instead of applying the spur, when they wish to get in high.

In the field of amateur athletics activities are fairly kaleidoscopic during the summer months. There are baseball teams, track teams, basket ball teams, tennis teams, etc., world without end, the strenuous life appealing to a large part of the citizenship. In the face of these conditions the Chess and Checker Club leads a retiring and almost shamefaced existence, with a membership of less than two dozen.

CHAPTER IX

GRAVE AND GAY IN POLITICS

THOUGH Birmingham is strongly Democratic in county, state and national elections, partisanship plays no part in municipal contests. With the substitution of the Commission Plan of Government for the Aldermanic System in 1910, ward lines disappeared, and party lines ceased to be drawn. Today nominations for commissioner are by petition, and party conventions, party primaries and party caucuses are made unlawful. The names of all nominees are placed on the same ballot, alphabetically arranged, and emblems of every kind and character are eliminated.

While the introduction of this system was a bitter pill to the old-time politician, and sporadic agitation was carried on for a time with a view of restoring the old order, the general satisfaction was such that no progress was made, and now one rarely hears the subject mentioned. The old guard died hard and died game — but died; died beyond the hope of resurrection.

It is an odd coincidence that one of the greatest apostles of low tariff in America came from Birmingham, a center where is produced vast quantities of the things for which the high tariff advocates demand protection. Oscar W. Underwood, author of the Underwood Tariff, and now Democratic leader in the Senate, is a Birmingham man. Not only so, but he is allied with one of the greatest iron producing agencies in the Alabama field. Yet, when the measure that bears his name was being framed, and tremendous pressure was brought upon him to "give his district some protection," he stood by his guns, and put through his own ideas of what a tariff law should be. The answer, from a political standpoint, is found in the fact that, whereas he was in the House, now he is in the Senate.

Another distinguished national leader whose home is in Birmingham is W. P. G. Harding, Governor of the Federal Reserve Board. His fame as a financier was won as the head of the largest bank in this city. He was succeeded here by Oscar Wells, who is now engaged in helping the Government of Cuba straighten out its financial system.

James J. Davis, Secretary of Labor in the Cabinet of President Harding, also lived in Birmingham at one time, being employed in what is popularly referred to as "the old rolling mill." That ancient enterprise, whose prosperity was a sure index of the prosperity of the city some thirty years ago, long since became obsolete and joined the things that were.

While Birmingham taboos partisan politics as it relates to municipal affairs, this city is the political center of the State, and here many dramatic events of national interest have been staged.

It was here that the effort to build up a strong Republican Party in the South was launched under the first Roosevelt administration. That abortive effort was known as the "Lily White" movement, and its rise and fall forms an interesting but little known chapter in the political history of the South and the Nation.

Because of his magnetic qualities, and the strong appeal his virile personality made to the average Southerner, it was believed by many leading Republicans of the South that a really strong organization could be built up in this section under the leadership of Mr. Roosevelt, provided the negro could be discarded. With this end in view, State leaders decided to start a movement looking to an all-white party.

Before calling the convention in Birmingham at which the new movement was to be launched, the leaders felt their way with care, and it is certain that they believed they had the approval of President Roosevelt before they took decisive action. Once they felt that the administration was behind them, they proceeded with great boldness and made a thorough job of reading the negro out of the party in this State. "Not a black face present" was the slogan of the occasion, and the spirit of this slogan was carried out to the letter.

This first and only "Lily White" convention was held in the armory of the City Hall, and not a negro was admitted, though many applied as in former years when state conventions were in progress, and there is little doubt that most of those applicants were accredited delegates.

The "key-note" speaker at this convention was the late Senator Pritchard, of North Carolina, who was received as the "spokesman" of President Roosevelt. He gave his unqualified endorsement to the idea of building up a strong Republican party in the South by creating conditions under which the Southern white man would feel free to unite with the organization, and what he had to say was listened to as coming from the President himself.

The men who dominated the convention were Federal officeholders, and that they would have thrown the negro overboard without being sure that they had executive approval is unbelievable. Yet, within a few weeks, every act of that convention was repudiated at Washington, and the prime movers in it were removed from office. And hereon hangs a tale that is not without its element of irony!

By some queer freak of chance it happened that a large gathering of negro churchmen was in session in Birmingham on the very day that the "Lily White" convention was held. Present were colored Bishops and other dignitaries from all over the country, including the big, important and politically doubtful states of the middle West. When these churchmen read in the afternoon papers that a Republican convention had that day been held in the city of Birmingham, right under their noses, as it were, and that not a negro had been admitted, their indignition was boundless. They felt that Greenland's Icy Mountains and the islands of the sea could wait for the nonce, while they attended to some missionary work at home, and straightway they trained their guns on Washington.

Returning to their respective homes, the Bishops, ministers, secretaries, etc., carried the news of what had happened in Alabama, and in a few days delegations of dusky individuals were marching upon the National Capitol, all thirsting for revenge. Heavy rumblings came from doubtful states, and presently the axe fell in Alabama. And to add to the humiliation of the gentlemen who had engineered the convention and thereby lost their jobs, a man who had stood alone in defense of the negroes was made Collector of Internal Revenue and Referee of Federal patronage in the State.

So the "Lily White" movement, like the grass of the field, blossomed forth in the morning, and in the evening was cut down. And thus died the movement to have a formidable Republican Party in the South.

That there is not a strong Republican organization in Birmingham, where one naturally would expect to find a pronounced protective sentiment, on account of the huge investments in industrial lines, is a matter of frequent comment on the part of national leaders of the Republican persuasion, upon their visits to this district. Vice-President Fairbanks was present on an occasion when this subject came up, and was much amused at a story told by Bishop Hoss, a distinguished figure in the Southern Methodist Church.

The occasion was a dinner at the Country Club tendered in honor of the Vice-President. He and Bishop Hoss had been friends for years, which accounted for the liberty the Bishop took in telling the story, which ran something like this:

In a small Southern city where nearly everybody belonged to the Methodist Church and the Democratic Party, a well known but somewhat erratic citizen created a sensation by quitting the Methodist Church and going over to the Universalist. There was a lot of gossip about it, but the talk finally subsided, and public thought was turning to other matters, when the same man threw the community into another furor by quitting the Democratic Party and going over to the Republicans.

While the gossip created by this incident was at its height, and the gentleman in question was being criticised rather severely by one of his fellow-townsmen, a local philosopher arose to remark: "Well, I don't blame him for this latest change. If I didn't believe there was a hell I'd be a Republican too!"

No man around the banquet board enjoyed this story more than Mr. Fairbanks.

The Vice-President was in Birmingham at that

time to deliver an address before a distinguished gathering of Southern Methodists, and earlier in the day he had created a perfect gale of laughter by an unconscious slip of the tongue.

Tall, dignified and immaculately clad, the Vice-President was introduced to the great gathering, representing the cream of Methodism in the South, and the laughter was occasioned when he opened his address by greeting this audience as "Fellow Republicans." For a moment he did not realize what the laughter was about, but upon recalling his opening sentence he joined in the general merriment.

Talk to a Birmingham man about amusing incidents in the field of politics, and he will be sure to relate this story about former Congressman Jesse Stallings and Judge William Brandon. The voice of the latter has been heard in more than one Democratic National Convention. And the term "heard" is used advisedly, for he has a voice that may not always carry conviction but which always carries far. A number of years ago the two were stumping the State for rival candidates for some position of preferment, and they happened to meet in a little town near which both were to speak at an all-day picnic. Stallings had obtained a buggy and was preparing to leave for the scene of festivities when he observed the presence of Brandon and invited him to go along. Brandon accepted the invitation, and while they were driving along Stallings, a great wag, happened to observe that Brandon wore a pair of striped silk hose.

When the speechmaking started that afternoon, Stallings was first introduced, and he began by paying the customary tribute to the beauty and charm of the womanhood of that particular section and to the intelligence, patriotism and loyalty of the men. Then he turned his guns to the opposition and wound up by pointing to Brandon and saying, "and now they send this city dude down here to tell you wool-hat boys, you rock-ribbed Democrats, how to vote. I want you to look at his socks; silk socks they are, striped like a stick of candy. Look at them!" and with that he stepped over and pulled up one of the legs of Brandon's trousers. But instead of the silk hose he exposed a bare ankle. Brandon, noting the way in which Stallings had eyed those hose, had taken time by the forelock and stuffed them in his shoes.

Stallings was rendered speechless for the first time in his life, and was ready to quit the game for the day, when Brandon arose and in tremulous tones began: "My fellow Citizens: I think things have reached a pretty pass in Alabama when a poor country boy can't come out on an occasion of this kind and talk to his people without having some city fellow make fun of his poverty." The honors of the occasion were his.

Brandon, by the way, tells a story illustrative of Alabama's greatness that has become a classic.

According to this story, an Alabama farm boy who came into the possession of some money decided to tour the old world and see if anywhere on the globe there was a spot half so favored as his native State, but while he traveled far and observed much, he saw nothing to compare with the wonders at home. No matter what he was shown, he always had something more remarkable to refer to in "Old Alabama." After seeing and discounting the marble quarries, the coal deposits and other natural resources of the Old World, he was carried to Birmingham, England, and permitted to view that great industrial city. Gazing upon it, he said, "There ain't none of you fellows ever been down to Birmingham, Alabama, has you?" When they replied "No," he said, "Then you don't know what an industrial town is. Why, there in Birmingham the smoke of industry is so thick that you can't recognize your best friend on the street."

Before the excursion of this Alabama booster was over, he was taken one night to the catacombs, this after he had been entertained at a function where flowed that which can't flow under the Eighteenth Amendment, and there he was left among the dead of bygone generations. The next morning, as faint rays began to creep into the gloomy cells, the lad awoke. In front of him he saw a skeleton, and glancing backward he saw another. Looking to left and to right he saw others. Then leaping to his feet and yelling in a voice that made those dreary chambers ring, he exclaimed: "It's the resurrection morn; I'm the first man up; Old Alabama leads again!"

During the past twenty-five years most of the political revolutions in Alabama have had their inception in Birmingham. Here originated the fight to rid the State of railroad dominance, and here that memorable campaign was directed. It was also from this city that the fight to rid the State of the saloon was carried on, and it was here that the stage was set for introducing the present constitution, under which the State was freed from the menace of negro dominance.

Until the adoption of this constitution in 1901, Alabama had been under an organic law framed in the days of "carpet-bag" rule, with the result that the ignorant colored voter was in the majority in many sections. The white man refused to be controlled by this situation, and it is an open secret that the ballot of the black man, though cast for the Republican candidate, usually came out as a vote for the Democratic nominee. Purloining of ballots and falsification of election returns were common offenses. The purchase of votes was a familiar occurrence, and it was not unusual for negroes to sell out to both sides. For instance, I recall a heated campaign in which the issue was so doubtful that every vote was considered highly important. Residing near the county site was an aged darky who had six sons, and it was the custom of the old man to bring his family to town on election day and drive the best bargain he could for the votes he controlled.

On the day in question the thrifty negro found a "bull" market and decided to sell when he was made what seemed to be a liberal offer. Upon selling out he started to the polls with his flock, but was met by the manager of the other candidate, who promptly opened negotiations.

"Uncle, how much do you want for your votes?" he was asked.

"I's sorry, boss," the darky replied, "but I's done fixed it up with the other gen'man."

"How much did you get?" he was asked.

"Fifteen dollars," was the reply, and the darky displayed three five dollar bills, which he held in his hand.

"I'll tell you what I'll do," said the crafty manager, "I'll just make it twenty dollars if you'll vote for my man."

The old negro hesitated and was lost. "Well, I got to do the best I can for my fam'ly, an' the votes is youn'."

Thereupon the manager slapped a five dollar bill upon the three the darky held in his hand, "making it twenty," and marched the old man and his sons up to the ballot box.

Both sides knew that this sort of thing was going on, and both sides "deplored" the condition, but, they asked, "What are we going to do about it so long as we have an electorate like this?"

The answer came in 1901 when the new constitution was adopted, and the negro disappeared as a factor in Alabama politics. This constitution contains the famous "grand-father" clause, the "education qualification," the "property qualification," the "optional poll-tax," and every other feature that could be devised for putting the colored voter on the retired list, without disfranchising the white man. It was an ingenious document, and effective beyond the dreams of those who framed it.

The black vote was wiped out under the educational clause, and was kept out by the optional-tax clause. The former made it possible to disfranchise any person who could not explain any clause of the United States Constitution about which he might be questioned, and the latter put it up to the individual to pay his poll tax voluntarily or lose his vote. Moreover, this poll tax had to be paid far in advance of the time of election, and it was not possible to qualify during the heat of a campaign by paying back taxes.

The effect of this not only was to disfranchise about ninety-five per cent of the negroes, but to disfranchise tens of thousands of whites. Illiterate whites could side-step the "educational qualification" under the provision of the "grandfather" clause, which conferred the ballot upon the sons and grandsons of soldiers who had fought in any war in which the United States had been involved, but he, too, was negligent in the matter of poll tax, and this proved his undoing. Today the total vote in Alabama never equals ten per cent of the population.

But this constitution, imperfect as it is, brought about a far-reaching reform, and elections now are as clean as the average, with many safeguards thrown about the ballot that were unknown in the old days. Moreover, there has developed a public sentiment that will not tolerate practices once justified under the stress of apparent necessity.

The new constitution was not framed in harmony, as Frank S. White, ex-United States Senator from Alabama, and a number of other able leaders, opposed the "grand-father" clause, which afterwards was the occasion of much ridicule, but the convention was dominated by the purpose to get rid of the negro, a purpose with which they sympathized, and nothing was left undone that promised to contribute to this end, however great the cost.

Because of the dominence of this idea, many important matters were neglected, and the result is that there is a growing demand for revision. This demand has been intensified during the past few months by the fact that a half dozen important amendments have been declared invalid, and it is probable that the next legislature, which convenes in 1923, will authorize a call for a convention charged with the duty of framing a new constitution.

Owing to the "one-idea" in the last convention, and the fear that too many changes might defeat the whole proposition, a large part of the former constitution was brought forward in the new, and this is proving a tremendous handicap to the State. The old constitution framed in 1876, also was put together in a one-idea atmosphere. Then the dominating thought was to keep the "carpet-bagger," who controlled the political situation in many communities, from getting his hands on any more of the public money than was necessary. The most stringent restrictions were imposed in matters of taxation, and these restrictions, brought over in 1901 by a convention that was chiefly concerned about the negro vote, have hindered progress. Educational advancement, harbor improvement, highway building, river development, and many more activities have been more or less throttled, though two amendments have been put through that proved of tremendous advantage in the promotion of the public schools.

All these matters will clamor for attention when the next convention assembles, and there is ground for hope that within the next few years a new constitution will be provided under which existing restrictions will disappear and Alabama will be enabled to exercise a large degree of freedom in the development of her rich and varied resources.

CHAPTER X

TURNING ORE INTO SHIPS

MOST of the scars left by the War between the States have vanished, but not all. For instance, one may see a deep crevasse running for miles along the crest of Red Mountain, that was dug during that unhappy struggle, and which continues to be a source of trouble and expense.

This rent was made in removing the "outcropping" of ore when the Conferedate Government was clamoring for iron with which to make cannon and other implements of warfare, and the operators, if they realized the damage they were doing, were too much occupied in meeting problems to worry about the future.

A fairly accurate conception of the structure of

Red Mountain may be gained by taking the two hands and bringing the ends of the fingers together in a straight line. Imagine the fingers, which are held level, to be a far-reaching bed of iron ore. Now, instead of holding the fingers straight, let them move upward, points together, until they form a peak like the roof of a house. When the reader has done this, he has seen in miniature what happened to the ore bed here many centuries ago. From a level plane, it was shot up to a peak, the peak becoming Red Mountain.

Now it obviously was a very simple matter for the men of 1861-65 to mine ore. All they had to do was to gather the outcropings at the top of the mountain, and that's what they did. Following the crest of the mountain, they went mile after mile, digging down fifteen, twenty or thirty feet, as the fancy struck them, and hauling off such ore as they wanted. This process involved no expensive shafts, no lifting machinery and no danger. Picks, shovels, and some blasting powder, and a few mules and carts, constituted the equipment necessary to gather this surface ore.

This system was very fine for the iron-makers of that period, but it laid up endless trouble for those who came later. That great trench, left when the old-timers tore the roof off the mountain, formed a natural catch-basin for all the rain the heavens were disposed to send down, and this water, having no natural outlet, takes a running start for every mine that is opened, and leaps therein, unless extraordinary precautions are adopted.

Nor was the creation of a serious water problem the only flare-back from this crude system of mining. The removal of the natural roof of the mountain created a weakness that is made manifest at every mine opening. Above these openings, one can see where the mountain has "cracked," and made ready to slide into the slope, and it has required vast quantities of cement and numberless timbers, to prevent this unhappy culmination.

Had the top of this mountain been left intact, it would have shed the water, and would have stood up reasonably well under the strain of mining activities. But, as indicated in the foregoing, the men who peeled off that top ore and left this legacy of trouble had neither the time nor the money to sink shafts. They were bending every energy to the task of "licking the Yankees," and the troubles of future mining engineers bothered them no whit.

The explorations made into Red Mountain since modern mining operations began, sustain fully the theory of early geologists that the Birmingham ores once were a mile or more below the surface of the earth, for there are a number of shafts now in operation that have a depth in excess of a mile, and the end is not yet. Somewhere down there, some day, the seams of ore, which now rise like the slate on the roof of a house, will straighten out, and then these bold explorers of the underworld will know how deep the top of Red Mountain used to be buried when the earth was young and men had not learned the value of poking experimental fingers into its interior.

Ore mines are numerous along Red Mountain, particularly in the vicinity of Birmingham and Bessemer. Muscoda furnishes a typical illustration of the methods used in the recovery of the material; methods that differ materially from those adopted in fields where the ore is deposited in "beds" from which it may be gathered by means of steam shovels. Here the ore veins are followed deep into the earth, which necessitates a main shaft for bringing the ore to the surface. From this shaft laterals are run, as in coal mining. The difference is that in ore mining, the men work "backward" instead of "forward," as in mines where the vein follows a level course.

This variation in the method of working is due to the "tilt" of the ore, and to the disposition of the operator to take advantage of every short cut. By going forward and working backward, he is enabled to get the benefit of a free haul, since the ore, when it is cut, rolls of its own momentum down to the lateral, and is ready to be hauled to the main shaft. Were it worked the other way about, it would have to be lifted to the lateral, instead of tumbling down of its own weight.

The use of the word "vein" in referring to deposits of coal and ore, has created the impression in the minds of some people outside the mining districts of the country, that these minerals are strung out like the veins in the human body. This impression is wholly erroneous, these deposits being in the form of "layers," and often covering wide areas. The method of recovering the mineral is to sink a shaft into the layer, wide enough and high enough to carry the cars in which the material is taken to the surface. From this main shaft, lateral openings are run at right angles through the coal or ore deposit, and the mine is worked from these laterals. In some instances, as in many coal mines, a sufficient amount of the mineral is left to support the roof, while in others all the coal is taken and the roof is supported by timbers. Then there are cases in which, after a mine has been worked, pillars of coal having been left as supports, the pillars are taken out and the roof is allowed to cave in.

Water, as may be inferred by any one who has seen a well dug and observed the ease with which water is "struck" under ordinary conditions, is one of the commonest problems confronting the mining engineer. For every ton of coal mined, it is necessary to pump from two to a dozen or more tons of water, depending upon the nature of the surroundings. Thus the removal of water becomes an important factor in the production of coal as well as of ore.

At Muscoda mine, the opening is made squarely into the side of the great trench left by the war-time operators as they dug away the outcroppings. There is a double shaft, protected by heavy arches of concrete that extend deep into the earth. Extending upward from this concrete work, two cracks in the mountain show where it made a futile attempt to drop down and block the entry. That concrete literally is holding the mountain up.

Two tracks drop into this slope, which is more than a mile deep. These tracks carry large trip cars, one of which goes down as the other comes up. One car balances the other, the result being that the weight of the ore is all the engines have to lift.

When the ore reaches the tipple above the opening of the shaft, it is dumped automatically into the crusher. From the crusher, it falls by gravity into the railroad cars, and is transported to the furnace.

As illustrating how blithesomely these mining men go about their tasks of mastering difficulties, it may be related that when it was decided to widen this slope sufficiently to care for two tracks instead of one, the man in charge of the undertaking carried the work forward a total distance of 380 feet in sixty days, meanwhile holding the mountain up with temporary timbers. By this feat he won a suit of clothes, not to mention such glory as comes with the achievement of large things.

Incidentally, there is nothing about these industrial enterprises more inspiring than the enthusiasm with which the dominating spirits jump to the performance of extraordinary tasks in the face of seemingly insurmountable difficulties. Some time ago fire destroyed the huge switchboard from which the operations of the great steel plant at Ensley were directed. The chaos in that electric room was frightful to behold, and it looked like a shut-down of from thirty to sixty days, as a new switchboard would have to be ordered from a distance, and no one could tell when delivery would be made. In this emergency, the presiding genius of the huge establishment

STEAMSHIP FABRICATED IN BIRMINGHAM

got his electricians together and had a wooden switchboard in commission in about thirty-six hours, whereupon the wheels began turning as usual. "It can be done," is a motto posted in practically all these establishments, and the spirit of that bold challenge permeates the district.

The furnaces and mills at Ensley may be seen from the ore mines along Red Mountain, and that is the destination of the ore when it tumbles into the cars from the crusher. Reaching the furnaces, this ore meets the coal that comes down from the mines at Bayview, Edgewater and other points, now appearing in the form of coke, and the two go into the furnace together.

When the ore is converted into "pig" by the heat of the burning coke, ore and coal meet again, this time in the steel mill, where the ore has become iron and the coal has become gas. Here the iron is transformed into steel, in which form it moves on to be converted into various products in the mills that reach out for miles beyond the steel plant. And all the way the transformed coal follows the transformed ore, in one form or another.

The far-reaching plant of the American Steel & Wire Company is one of the first in the chain of giant industries lying beyond the Ensley Steel Mill, while farther along are the great buildings constituting the plant of the Fairfield Steel Company. Here the ore from Red Mountain appears in the form of the steel "ingots," some of them as much as 48 inches wide and weighing 22,000 pounds.

These "ingots" pass first into the furnace room, where the high temperature generated by the gas that used to be coal, brings them to a white heat. In this form, they are carried by giant electric cranes to the blooming mill, where they pass between great rolls and gradually are reduced to such form as is required to meet pending orders.

It is here that the steel plates are rolled for the building of the ships that are fabricated in the nearby plant of the Chickasaw Shipbuilding & Car Company, and for the steel cars manufactured in the same establishment.

This mill produces rails, bars and structural material, and is as spectacular in its operations as any enterprise in the district. The rolls produce sheets of steel as much as 110 inches wide, and to see them kneading one of those great, hot ingots into long strips of metallic "dough," ready to be cut into "wafers" for boiler heads, or attenuated "lady fingers" for ship sides, is an awe-inspiring spectacle.

The machinery is all electrically driven, the rolls being connected directly upon the shafts of motors.

The largest of these motors develops five thousand four hundred horse power, its function being to reduce the great mass of steel as it comes from the mill. Smaller motors, of three thousand, twenty-five hundred and one thousand horse power, care for the subsequent operations.

All parts of this wide-spread plant are reached by underground passages of concrete, large enough to operate a mine train through, and all of the electric cables traverse these tunnels. Tiled, lined, and spotless, and with electrical machinery shining like mirrors, the power plants are veritable beauty spots.

Beyond the blooming mill is the plate fabricating shop, and adjoining that is the tie plate plant, where automatic machinery works with red hot metal as though it knew all about the job in hand. The strips of metal are fed into its maw direct from the furnace, and it chews away as long as the feeding process continues, spilling the finished product in a convenient hopper.

Beyond the plant of the Fairfield Steel Company is that of the Chickasaw Shipbuilding & Car Company, consisting of a series of huge steel structures, fabricated in the plant of the Fairfield Company. Here is witnessed one of the most remarkable transformations wrought in the Birmingham district, for it is at this plant that ocean steamships are turned out, ready to be put together and launched at Mobile.

This development is interesting, not only because of the magnitude of the operation, but because of its significance, since it is here that the circle of Birmingham's industrial accomplishment is made complete. The ore, starting from Red Mountain, passes through furnaces and mills and fabricating plants, emerging finally as an ocean-going craft, prepared to convey the products of Birmingham anywhere upon the seven seas.

Operations here are upon a colossal scale. Huge shafts of steel, destined for ship propellers, turn in giant lathes, mighty hammers pound upon forgings that weigh many tons, great sheets of plate steel pass beneath restless punching machines, while overhead electric cranes move back and forth, conveying materials whose weight runs into tens of thousands of pounds.

When the ship has been completed, ready to be put together with the seven hundred and fifty thousand steel rivets which go with the parts, the whole is sent to Birminghamport, where self-propelled steel barges carry it to the ship yard at Mobile. Every part is punched and marked, showing exactly where it goes, and it remains only for these parts to be riveted together. Steel cars form another important item in the product of this plant, the capacity being one completed car every forty-eight minutes.

The building in which the cars are put together is ninety feet wide and one thousand and eighty feet long. The materials for building the cars are piled at stations all along the length of this shop, and at each station certain operations are performed. Men and materials are so arranged that each operation, in the building of the car, consumes forty-eight minutes. When the trucks roll in at the far end of the shop, the first crew adds certain elementary features, and the car moves on; the second crew adds other parts, and so the car progresses until it emerges at the far end, with every steel part riveted in place. Under this schedule a car is produced every forty-eight minutes.

While most of the machinery in these buildings is of colossal proportions, designed to handle enormously heavy materials, there are many smaller machines, busily engaged in turning out nuts, bolts and products of like character.

About these shops is the same evidence of appreciation of the beautiful that is found in the mining camps to which reference has been made. As one enters the great enclosure containing the buildings, he beholds a wide semi-circle of green, which was aglow with blooming flowers the day of my visit. About the office buildings, and wherever the space seems to be available, similar flower beds are placed. Here, too, ice water, from sanitary drinking fountains, is abundant, and the shops are provided with ample facilities for the personal comfort of the men. Narrow strips of steel and great stretches of glass, form the architectural scheme of the buildings, and light and air have free access.

The opportunity to lend ornamentation to these vast structures of steel is very limited, but not so with the power plants, and here elegance is the dominant note. Indeed, when one considers how rare it is that outsiders see the inside of one of these establishments, it is to marvel that so much should be spent in making them places of beauty. In these plants, as in many others, the decorative scheme in the power houses is a border of white tile, extending to a height of about six feet, while above this, polished brick, of a rich sand color, extends to the ceiling. Red tile floors furnish a striking contrast to the deep green of the huge electric machines, and the effect is dignified and pleasing.

Fairfield, an industrial community noted for its beauty, is the home of most of the white employees of these plants, while Westfield, a model negro community, is the home of the colored employees.

Here are found neat homes, splendid streets, a modern school, an athletic field, and many other features that go to make an attractive community.

In consideration the completeness of residence sections like Westfield, I am reminded of the story of the negro evangelist who put new life into a rather indifferent congregation. This evangelist, as the story goes, was a powerful " 'zorter," and he hadn't been preaching long until the congregation was willing to do anything he suggested. As a result, the church was painted and a new roof was put on. Then a new carpet was added, and some stained glass windows were put in. Following this, the congregation, swayed by the eloquence of the evangelist, bought a pipe organ and added new pews to the church equipment, thus giving what seemed to be the final touch to the edifice. But the end was not yet, for presently, under the inspiring call of the preacher for sacrificial service, one good brother arose and said "Brethren, now that we've done had our church painted an' got new windows an' a carpet, an' has installed a musical organ of de fustest class, I now moves dat we completes de job by buyin' a nice chandeliar."

Thereupon an aged brother, seated in the "amen corner," arose and remarked: "Sisters an' bredeeren: I's voted for de paint an' de carpet, an' for de benches an' de organ, but I'm here to tell you now I'm not gwin' to have nothin' to do with no sech plan as am now perposed. I'm again' buyin' no chandeliar, for if we had one there wouldn't be a nigger in dis house would know how to play it!"

That's the way with Westfield, and similar communities. If any features were added to these communities, it is probable that the folks wouldn't know what to do with them, because things are complete as they stand.

CHAPTER XI

CONSERVING THE HUMAN ELEMENT

STANDING upon an eminence, and almost surrounded by a huge artificial lake that forms a sweeping crescent, is Bayview, the most modern of all the mining villages in the Birmingham district.

Viewing this village, with its wide stretches of grass, its riot of blooming flowers, its winding thoroughfares, its playgrounds, and its scores of artistic homes, my thoughts ran back to other scenes that left their impress some twenty-five or thirty years ago. I could see a mining camp stuck in a narrow valley, the hillsides dotted with rough-board shacks, whose spindly legs seemed ever on the eve of giving way. Rough trails led from shack to shack, and fell toward the "town," whose single street was filled with either dust or mud, according to the eccentricities of the weather. No flowers, no parks, no playgrounds, no public baths; nothing save ugliness and the evidence of grinding toil. That was the beginning, production of coal being the only thought. Today, at Bayview, and many other villages, one sees the practical working of a new idea; the idea that a mining camp ought to be a home as well as a hive of industry.

Another picture, connected with that early camp, comes back upon the screen of memory, and it, too, is suggestive of the mighty change that has been wrought in the social order.

In those days the women and the children of the camp had no recreation, and that toward which some of the men turned, called for cork-screws or bung-starters rather than for tennis rackets or baseball bats. I recall two brothers, stocky, powerful fellows, who used to go to town as regularly as they were paid off, and who always returned with a gallon jug of liquor, each being so armed against the possibility of drouth between pay days. On one occasion, as they stepped from the train and started down the track, they staggered toward one another, and as they did, the jugs crashed together, with the result that all the liquor was lost. Each accused the other of carelessness, and the upshot of the altercation was a fight that furnished vast amusement to the spectators.

Scenes like this were familiar, as was the sight of a mountain of beer kegs piled up about the station, "empties" going back to take the place of the full kegs coming in.

Scenes more sordid than these, or more detrimental to the development of a home life characterized by social and intellectual progress, one scarcely could imagine, and there is nothing in the development of the Birmingham district that is more inspiring, or better calculated to imbue the human race with hope, than the transformations being wrought in mining communities.

Advantages such as are offered in the Bayview type of village are equalled in few small communities, and not many resorts of the wealthy have a more delightful setting.

The central feature of this village is a beautiful office building, looking not unlike a well-designed public library. There are three entrances, one being marked by a neat pergola, and all being flanked by flowers and shrubs. Stretching off from the right wing, three flower beds, radiant with color on the July day upon which I visited the place, point the way to the huge black tipple that looms above the mouth of the mine. This tipple, by the way, is the only "manless" device of its kind in Alabama. The coal, coming up from the slope, is dumped automatically, six tons at a load, and is conveyed through crushers, washers and to cars by mechanical means.

On one side of the village is the white settlement, while on the other side is the negro quarter. The central feature of both sections is a beautiful school house, each a duplicate of the other. These buildings, in addition to the usual class of rooms, have large halls for concerts, dances, dramatic performances, religious services and public meetings, and also are provided with small libraries for general use.

These residential communities are circled by well paved streets, which follow the contour of the hills, the streets being flanked by homes that are wonderfully neat and attractive. Most of the homes have four rooms, but there is little uniformity in construction. Each is so designed that it has features distinctive from its neighbor, but all set back an equal distance from the street, being separated by a wide stretch of lawn. Shrubbery abounds, and during the summer months there is a perfect riot of flowers about the porches and windows of these homes. The shrubbery is planted by the company, but the flowers are furnished by the families occupying the homes, and the abundance of blossoms bears witness to the zeal of the householders in the matter of beauty.

One of the most attractive tennis courts in Alabama adjoins the white school, and there is also a well appointed court for the public, in addition to a large athletic field. This field, though quite a distance from the heart of the village, is reached by a paved road, flanked by a concrete walk.

The crescent lake is compassed by high and heavily wooded bluffs as a rule, the village being about a hundred feet above the water level. Splendid bathing facilities are afforded, and there are some beautiful scenes along the lake. This lake is the chief source of supply for many of the great industries of the Tennessee Company in and about Ensley, and was provided for this purpose by the construction of a ninety-foot dam of concrete. Furnaces, mills, coal washers and the like consume an immense quantity of water, and every effort is made to conserve this very necessary product. Water pumped from mines is brought into service, and many ingenious methods are adopted in making the same water serve over and over again. Even the water which drips from coal cars, where freshly washed coal has been loaded, is caused to run into depressions, from which it is carried back to serve in washing more coal.

Water for human consumption is also provided in the greatest abundance. Sanitary drinking fountains, from which ice cold water is drawn, are found at convenient points in and about every plant where men are employed. For this purpose City of Birmingham water is provided, coming through pipes which are coiled through underground ice chests.

In Bayview the dispensary, a neat brick building, stands upon a knoll, and here one may observe some interesting and enlightening incidents; incidents which graphically illustrate how the new order has succeeded the old. It is much more than a place for giving treatment to such as may be injured. Here a "baby clinic" is conducted every Thursday, the tots of the community being weighed and examined to see just how they are faring since coming "out of the nowhere into the here." Nutrition classes also are conducted regularly, and the children brought into this class are watched with the greatest care. The utmost co-operation exists between the health department and the schools, and children brought into the nutrition class are given close supervision in the school room. If the physician prescribes an hour of rest at a certain time during the day, the teacher sees that the child is snugly laid away for this hour. Meanwhile the progress of the child in the home is watched by the woman visitor, who works in co-operation with the camp physician.

Whether it is the romantic setting, or the presence of an unusually appreciative people, that causes the drama to flourish so in this community, I know not, but the fact is that here the art finds expression in many excellent performances, and enjoys a patronage that truly is remarkable.

The fame of the dramatic organization of Bayview is known throughout the Birmingham district, and each winter the club goes over a regular circuit, giving entertainments in other villages. In this wise the joy and the inspiration of the drama is spread abroad.

Viewing what is going on at Bayview, and in other well appointed industrial communities, I wonder at the persistence of the word "camp," a term used by about nine out of ten persons in referring to these villages. "Camp" suggests something rough and transitory; a sort of temporary make-shift, and nothing more misleading could be imagined when applied to such places as these; places where permanency is suggested at every turn; by well paved streets, by concrete sidewalks, by splendid brick buildings, and by homes in which the occupants take the greatest delight in making the surroundings attractive. In the progress of industry in this district, "camp" has become a misnomer that should be erased.

Returning for a moment to the dispensary, it

may be observed that here is where the teeth of the community are kept in shape for the daily grind. A well equipped dental office is maintained, and the dentist drops in periodically, giving special attention to the children.

Reference has been made to the fact that the only "manless" coal tipple in Alabama, and probably in the South, is at Bayview. With the tipple, the crusher and the washer, all working automatically and forming a towering series of structures, it presents an impressive view, and bears eloquent testimony to the ingenuity shown by man in the elimination of grinding labor and in the promotion of safety.

And speaking of safety, it is a fact that one of these modern mines, with its multiplicity of devices for the prevention of accidents, is much safer than the average city street. Consider the matter of fresh air, which is essential to the well-being of the men who toil far down in the earth. At Bayview, and many other mines, a constant flow is insured by duplicate machinery and multiplied means of propulsion. Here the fans may be operated by three sources of power, all of which are instantly available. These include hydro-electric power, power generated in the local plant, and power furnished by steam. If any source of

HOMES OF MINERS IN MODERN VILLAGE

power fails, another is brought into action without a moment's loss of time.

A great concrete tunnel, arched and massive, and carrying two extra width railroad tracks, drops from the Bayview tipple to the loading level, hundreds of feet below. Steel cars move down this slope to what might aptly be termed a great railroad terminal; a point from which radiate all the lines that permeate the mine. As the loaded cars swing in from these diverse lines, they pass over the cars connected with the tipple, and are dumped automatically. As soon as a car is loaded, it runs to the surface, climbs the tipple, is dumped automatically, and drops back to receive another load. Meanwhile the coal which has just been delivered to the tipple is carried upon belt conveyors to the crusher, and thence to the washer, from which it falls into railroad cars that carry it to the coke oven. One man attends to the loading in the mine, and another operates the hoisting machinery, but this is the only labor involved until the coal reaches the washer.

A separate slope carries the miners in and out and conveys all the materials and supplies that go into the mine. No coal passes through it, while nothing but coal goes through the other slope. All of the machinery is electrically driven.

To follow a car of coal, as it moves from this

mine, furnishes an illuminating experience. It goes to the great by-product plant at Fairfield, where it passes into one of the many coke ovens. There it is subjected to hours of "cooking," gas accumulated from other loads of coal furnishing the fuel. When the tremendous heat has transformed the coal into coke, a giant engine, the essential feature of which is a lengthy "ram," moves up while another machine lifts the door off the furnace. Then the "ram," which conforms to the shape of the high and narrow oven, pushes the glowing mass out the other end of the oven, where it falls into a steel car, which moves slowly along in order that the seething mass may be evenly distributed as it tumbles out. This car is driven by an electric engine that looks much like a wartime "tank," this appearance being suggested by the way in which the engineer is housed about by steel, designed to protect him from the heat.

The car of red-hot coke is run into a shower, where it is cooled by the water, and then it is dumped upon a tilted platform of steel, down which it rolls to a belt conveyor and is carried off to furnish fuel for the huge battery of furnaces, where ore is being smelted into iron.

If one will picture in his mind a box such as the familiar Christmas neckties come in, and then multiply the size of this box scores of times, he may form a rough idea of the shape of these by-product coke ovens. High, narrow and deep, they stand side by side in long tiers. Over them may be observed certain pipes, and these pipes play a most important part in the performance. For the making of coke is but one of the functions of the coke oven. The other is to create gas.

In another chapter has been told the story of the great coal "tree;" showing how many and varied are the by-products of this wonderful mineral. Here one sees some of the processes by which these by-products are caught, "on the wing," as it were.

The gas, coming from the coke oven, is conveyed hither and yon, passing through a huge tank here, and a great vat there, and at every stage of the journey it is robbed of some element. It starts out like a beautiful bunch of grapes, but is picked on by one process after another until, you might say, nothing is left but the stem. Benzol, naphthalene, ammonium sulphate, ammonia and tar are the chief products at this plant, these products being susceptible to many transformations.

The processes are far too technical for the layman, but one cannot go over such a plant, so colossal in its proportions, without feeling an inclination to take his hat off to the men who devised such processes and achieved such amazing results.

This plant, a subsidiary of the United States Steel Corporation, adjoins the Ensley and Fairfield works, subsidiaries of the same organizations, and the gas, after being stripped, as above outlined, is piped to these plants, there to perform a multiplicity of service. Immense quantities are consumed in the process of converting iron into steel; in keeping white-hot the great furnaces in which slabs of steel, often weighing thousands of pounds, are heated for forging, and in many other operations. Steam has become obsolete in the Fairfield plants, gas and electricity furnishing the fuel and the power.

The attitude of the men about these plants forms an interesting study, and one cannot fail to be impressed by the feeling of proprietorship and the pride of performance which characterizes them. This is due in large part to the fact that the men, in many instances, actually own a part of the plant in which they work, a majority of the employees of the Steel Corporation being stockholders. As the jockey pats his horse, and tells marvelous tales of its feat upon the track, so these men, figuratively speaking, pat the giant machines with which they work and fill one's ears with such stories of accomplishments as seem almost unbelievable. But always the record is there to sustain them. However, your thoughts are not so much upon their words as upon the spirit that prompts the utterance. Why should a grimy figure upon the huge coal washer fill your ears with a wonderful story of what the washer is accomplishing, and be so eager to impress you with the idea that no other washer is quite so capable of doing the job? Or why should a furnace man, looking like a pigmy beside the towering stack, talk of that stack's performances as a father might boast of the accomplishments of a son? And the men at the coal mines and the ore mines, why their zeal to impress you with the idea that while other mines may have some very excellent appointments, their particular mine has this or that feature which places it a bit in the forefront?

I recall going through a factory big enough to cover a city block. It was at the close of the noon hour, and the machines, strung out in long lines, were just starting up. The superintendent stepped up to one of these machines and asked the stocky man in charge how soon it would be running. "In a minute," was the reply, the operator at the moment being engaged in oiling his machine. This done, he turned to the furnace that glowed beside him, and examined the sundry bars of steel that were being heated preparatory to working. Unhurried, he watched the rapid evolutions of his machine and the color of the steel, as the heat increased, and then, when everything was just right, he began to feed those ruddy bars into the hungry mouth of the hurrying machine, and nuts began to rain into a receptacle below it. Then, with a long pair of tongs, he picked up one of these nuts and passed it pridefully over to the superintendent in order that I might see at close range just what wonders his machine could accomplish.

Again I stood beside a man who operated a towering press engaged in shaping sheets of steel for use in building railroad cars. Amid the roar and din, he stopped to tell me that the machine would exert so many thousands of pounds of pressure — how many pounds, I do not recall, but I got the idea he wished to convey, which was that the machine before which I stood was in a class by itself. In this shop, more than a thousand feet in length, were other wonderful machines. Some could punch unprecedented numbers of holes in sheets of steel at one operation, and others could make record-breaking cuts when it came to trimming steel. And so it went, pride of performance cropping out at every turn.

Analyzing this evident feeling of proprietorship on the part of the men, and this feeling of manifest pride in the accomplishments made possible by modern methods, one is forced to the conclusion that co-operation between the company and the men in making the home life and the community life pleasant, has brought about a like measure of co-operation in the operation of the enterprises upon which the home and the community are founded. The company, co-operating with the men, seeks to make the home life pleasant; the men, co-operating with the company, seek to make the enterprise profitable. That's the way it seems to work, and that's the explanation of the tremendous expenditures for schools, for educational advantages, for recreational features, for amusements and the like.

Some of the industrial organizations which have been so active in making these communities attractive, and in giving every possible advantage to the employees, have been charged with harboring paternalistic tendencies, when the truth is that they have learned a new lesson in investment, and are putting their money into these things because it pays. They act upon the principle that "the quality of the product is a composite of the character of the men who make it."

Modern merchants do not provide wonderful window displays because they like to spend large sums for window-dressers, or to lend so much valuable space to the creation of a pleasing picture. They do it because it commands the attention and the admiration of people on the outside, and attracts them into the store, where they may become permanent contributors to the success of the establishment. Actuated by like motives, the far-seeing industrial organizations seek to make their villages sufficiently attractive to bring into them men who will become permanent contributors to the success of their enterprises.

CHAPTER XII

IRON FOR THE CONFEDERACY

THOUGH Birmingham had not come into existence at the time of the Civil War, the fact that the ingredients for iron making existed in this district was known years before that conflict, and when the Confederate Government began to manufacture implements of war, one of the first steps was to invade the mineral section of North Alabama for materials. Two furnaces were built within a few miles of the valley in which Birmingham is located, and here iron for the manufacture of cannon was turned out.

An arsenal was erected at Selma, and iron from this district was carried to that city to be converted into cannon. The furnaces from which this metal came were known as the Ironton furnace and the Irondale furnace. The former, first to be erected, had been in blast only a short time when it was put out of business by Wilson's riders. The latter, located in an almost inaccessible spot and difficult to find even today, being invisible until one is fairly upon it, escaped discovery and was in operation until the close of the war.

The Irondale furnace was built by W. S. McElwain, a New Englander by birth but an "unregenerated rebel" by inclination. He came to Alabama from Holly Springs, Miss., where he had operated a foundry that was busily engaged in manufacturing cannon, rifles, swords, shells and other implements of warfare for the Confederate Government.

When Mississippi was invaded by the Union forces, the plant of McElwain, which was credited with making the first cannon used by Confederate artillerymen, was destroyed and McElwain was forced to flee. Knowing something of the iron deposits in North Alabama, he came to this district, bought several hundred acres of land in the vicinity of Irondale, and at once built the furnace which stands there today. It served the Confederacy well, but remained idle for a long time after the close of the conflict between the states. However, in 1868, it was again put in blast, this time by an Ohio firm which began preparations for the erection of a rolling mill. The plan did not materialize, however, and the operation of the furnace finally was suspended. In 1871, the year of Birmingham's birth, a Pennsylvania firm acquired the property by lease, and operated it for some time.

Samuel Davis, who was connected with the Pennsylvania interests and who became intimately acquainted with the ancient Irondale furnace, through daily contact, now resides in New Jersey, where, when he learned that the property had been purchased by George Gordon Crawford, President of the Tennessee Coal, Iron & Railroad Company, he wrote an interesting description of the old-time plant and sent it to Mr. Crawford, together with a number of photographic views taken during the early days.

The furnace is an ordinary stone stack with four arches lined with red brick, having an open top and being about thirty feet square at the base. It is thirty-five feet high, and at that time was equipped with a single blowing engine. The output in the beginning was from five to seven tons per day, though this was increased somewhat by the installation of a hot blast. It is interesting to note in this connection that as much as 609 tons of iron have been produced in a single day at one of the huge furnaces in the Tennessee plant at

Ensley. The general superintendent of the plant was James Thomas, who afterwards became a large figure in the iron industry of Birmingham, and who is credited by Mr. Davis with being the first man to make Birmingham iron into pig by the coke process, this at the Oxmoor furnace in 1876.

The ore, brown hemetite, was mined about a mile and a half from the furnace and was carried to the furnace by gravity, the empty cars being carried back both by oxen and mule teams. The limestone was obtained in the same vicinity, and the fuel, wood, was cut within a radius of six miles, being reduced to charcoal in pits. A highly ingenious arrangement for hoisting the fuel was worked out. It was known as a "water hoist," and consisted of two water-tight compartments. When one of these compartments was flooded the fuel container went up; when the water was withdrawn, it came down! This neat arrangement worked in a highly satisfactory manner. The furnace helpers numbered about twenty, while wood-choppers, charcoal burners and teamsters numbered about thirty.

The Irondale furnace was abandoned finally in the early seventies, and is now a picturesque ruin. The furnace and the abandoned farm upon which it is located were purchased by Mr. Crawford largely through sentimental reasons. His ownership of a useless furnace and an abandoned farm has occasioned much friendly raillery by his friends, among whom speculation as to whether he would lose more money in operating the farm than he would in operating the furnace, continues even to this day.

The Ironton furnace, though destroyed in part by Union forces, was never abandoned. At the time of the founding of Birmingham it had been rebuilt, much of the money being provided by Daniel Pratt, the shrewd New Englander who had improved Eli Whitney's cotton gin and become rich through the operation of a gin factory at Prattville. As in many other enterprises in these days, the dominant spirits were ex-Confederate soldiers, Henry D. Clayton, Daniel S. Troy, H. F. DeBardeleben, all of whom had served the Confederacy and all of whom became historic figures in the State.

When Birmingham was founded, this furnace plant was operated by the Red Mountain Iron Company, which had acquired six thousand acres of land, including a large section of Red Mountain, and was actively engaged in trying to locate other furnaces in the vicinity. A New York newspaper of 1873 carried the announcement that this company would furnish locations for furnaces on their property "at a merely nominal figure," and "will then agree to furnish all the material for making iron, delivered at the furnace for $11 a ton for each ton of pig iron produced." The materials to be furnished for $11 were enumerated as follows:

2 tons iron ore.........	$1 50
1½ tons coke..........	9 00
Limestone	50

"Companies availing themselves of this opportunity," the announcement continued, "will escape much of the outlay attending the starting of an independent furnace." But the idea seemed not to have appealed very strongly to the furnace builders of that period, for while the time came when many new stacks were built in and about Birmingham, none arose to keep company with the pioneer at Ironton, now known as Oxmoor.

At the time the Red Mountain Iron Company, which long since passed out of existence, was attempting to bring other enterprises of like character into this district, and was offering to supply coke at $6 per ton, no process had been found for the successful conversion of Birmingham coal into coke, and the Ironton furnace was being operated with charcoal. But the men behind the enterprise had made up their minds that they were going to produce coke for iron making, and, to show that their hearts were in the right place, they offered freely to share the coke which was yet to be produced with other ironmakers, yet to be produced.

That the vast assurance thus displayed was justified in a measure, subsequent events proved. Yet the justification did not come forthwith. As a matter of fact, it was three years later before the first coke iron was made in Birmingham. But when finally it was produced it was produced at this very furnace. The story of how this triumph was achieved and its vast significance to the district, is told in another chapter.

The same metropolitan journal that carried the announcement of the furnace company, carried also an article by James R. Powell, "the Duke of Birmingham," in which he pictured the glories of the new city in language vibrant with the spirit of the times. Hear him:

"While other sections of the State, and of almost the entire South, have been oppressed by calamities, political and financial, consequent upon the war — our section, its healthful climate cheering the invalid — its fertile valleys tempting the agriculturist, and its pregnant mountains groaning to be delivered of their wealth, our favored section, the Eldorado of the iron-masters, soon to be penetrated by railroads from every point of the compass, invites with open arms and with full capacity to entertain them as congenial spirits—skilled labor, capital and intelligencé from every portion of the globe, affording opportunities and facilities to all to exercise their functions and endowments in their most agreeable vocations."

From the above paragraph, which is reproduced just as it appeared in New York on April 5, 1873, it requires no Sherlock to deduce that Colonel Powell thought right well of his little town. However, if additional evidence is needed, it may be found in a report he issued on January 25, 1872, and which also was published in New York, the title being "The Rise and Progress of Birmingham, Ala." To appreciate this title fully, one should remember that Birmingham had then been incorporated a fraction less than sixty days and that six months before an ancient blacksmith shop was the only building on the ground.

After pointing out the great embarrassment caused by the suspension of operations on the part of the Alabama and Chattanooga Railroad, and the failure of the South and North Railroad to begin regular operations until November, 1871, which condition made the procurement of lumber almost impossible, Colonel Powell proceeded:

"It is gratifying that, with all these embarrassing surroundings, Birmingham has grown from a barren waste to the proportions of a city in

five months from the commencement of the first building, with a population of from seven to eight hundred, drawn from the best material of this and adjoining states, and about 125 houses, all well built and of good material; among them are a railroad hotel with thirty-seven rooms, seventeen two and three story brick stores completed and in progress; about thirty-five frame stores of one and two stories; some sixty dwellings, many of them creditable to a city of much larger growth and maturer age; two planing mills, one in successful operation and another about ready to start, and one to manufacture sash, doors, blinds, etc.; two grist-mills in rapid progress of erection; one newspaper and job printing office; one extensive livery stable; five boarding houses; two bakeries and two restaurants, and all the other accompaniments to a thriving and progressive city, including express, telegraph and post-offices.

"In the proof of the rapid growth of the city, I will here state that so recently as August last, the present beautiful site of the central feature of the city was a low, flat marsh, covered with water and an almost impenetrable jungle of vines and trees."

The "central feature of the city" to which Colonel Powell referred was Lynn Park, then at the Southwest corner of First Avenue and Twentieth Street. This "low flat marsh" is the hub of Birmingham today, and the corner where grew the "almost impenetrable jungle," is described by the modern enthusiast as "the heaviest in the world." It is so designated because each corner of the intersection is occupied by a large office building, the aggregate height of the four being sixty-two stories. It was on one of these corners, now occupied by the largest office building in the South, that Charles Lynn, pioneer banker, erected what for that period was a building of unusual magnificence. He did this when Birmingham was in its swaddling clothes, and for several years the structure was pointed to as "Lynn's folly." It was an ornament to the city for over three decades, and then gave way to a sixteen-story structure containing over eight hundred offices.

Colonel Powell, as head of the pioneer Elyton Land Company, which founded Birmingham and steered it to permanency before passing from the stage, came forward in February, 1873, with another résumé of things accomplished, and with more buoyant prognostication of things to come. He said then:

"Our population now is about 4,000, with about 500 houses, of which fifty-four are brick or stone (none less than two stories high), and about 125 frame stores; the remainder consisting of about 250 neat and substantial brick and frame dwellings, six churches — which were erected by our own citizens almost entirely without assistance from abroad — two public halls, four hotels of from 10 to 30 rooms each, several private boarding houses and restaurants, a national bank in successful operation several manufacturing establishments, and all the other concomitants which go to make up a prosperous and thriving city."

The Birmingham described in this language was the Birmingham upon which the cholera epidemic laid its blight just four months after the words were written. The effect of the epidemic was to empty the stores and dwellings and to leave the little city prostrate, the high hopes of its people being crushed to earth for the time being.

Proceeding, Colonel Powell gave utterance to this significant paragraph:

"I can with pride point to our people as a bright exception to the general character of population forming new towns. Our churches attest that our people are moral and religious, and our city court records prove that crime is almost unknown among us."

The condition thus described did not continue, as lawlessness became rampant in latter years, but the religious and moral spirit to which he referred remained, and in the end it triumphed over the elements which, for a time, ran a riotous course. And the same fine spirit survives today—its presence proclaimed by many magnificent temples of worship, and by the high moral tone which characterizes the community.

The decade between 1880 and 1890 proved the golden age in furnace building in and about Birmingham. It having been demonstrated at the rejuvenated Oxmoor furnace that iron could be made of Birmingham ores, numerous furnace companies were organized and new stacks began to go up in all quarters. The Woodward Company, today one of the great industrial agencies in the district, erected two furnaces. The Alice Furnace Company built two, the Sloss Company, another present-day giant in the iron industry, erected two, subsequently acquiring two put up by the Coalburg Coal & Coke Company; the Mary Pratt Company put up one, the Williamson Company one, the Bessemer Company two, the Tennessee Company four, and the Pioneer Company two.

The output of these early furnaces ran as a rule between fifty and sixty tons per day, but in 1886 furnace No. 2 of the Sloss Company was proclaimed a record-breaker, having produced 150 tons within twenty-four hours. This was said to have been the greatest tonnage ever produced at a Southern furnace up to that time.

Since that date the breaking of records has been the usual thing in the Birmingham field. Furnaces were rebuilt as methods became obsolete and the necessity for increased production arose, with the result that the sites are about all that remain of the first iron-makers, enormous stacks standing where the small ones stood in the earlier days.

Reference has been made to the production of 609 tons of iron in a single day at the Ensley plant, where six giant furnaces stand today. Furnace No. 3 in this group holds the world's record for production without relining. It ran for ten years and five months, and produced a total of 1,429,000 tons of iron before operations had to be suspended in order to put in a new lining. No. 2 furnace, standing shoulder to shoulder with this record-breaker, ran it a remarkable race, going nine years and six months on the same lining, and producing 1,192,000 tons of iron before its interior had to be gone over.

The measure of progress indicated here applies to practically all the great iron producing agencies in the Birmingham district. The Tennessee Company, the Republic Iron & Steel Company, the Sloss Company and the Woodward Company all have kept pace with the industry, as they have in the production of coal and ore.

Recent years have brought tremendous advances in coke making, as well as in iron making. The old-fashioned bee-hive ovens, which made good coke but which lost all the highly valuable ingredients of the coal, have disappeared as a rule, most of the coke being produced today under conditions which make possible the salvaging of by-products that are of immense value, and which form the basis of many important industries throughout the district.

With the passing of the old-time coke ovens passed a picturesque feature from the local landscape. Arranged in long rows, like bee-hives, and with smoke and flame issuing from the circular opening at their peaks, they presented a remarkable spectacle to the uninitiated on entering the city at night. Their glare illumined the heavens, and their smoke gave to the atmosphere a pungent odor, somewhat suggestive of the lower regions. A lengthy battery of these ovens stood for years along the lines of certain railroads, and it was not an unusual thing to hear some visitor, arriving at night, exclaim that Birmingham might be a heavenly place in which to live, but it looked like h—— from a railroad train.

This particular battery of ovens belonged to the

Sloss Company, which since has erected an immense by-product plant outside the city limits. There it produces coke under conditions which admit of the recovery of many valuable by-products. It is from this plant that Birmingham receives its gas supply, both for cooking and illuminating purposes. The use of this by-product, which went to waste in old days, makes it possible for Birmingham citizens to get their gas for about half as much as is paid in communities where the old methods of gas production are in vogue.

It was the presence of this gas that brought the International balloon race of 1920 to Birmingham, and it was with this gas that Belgium captured the trophy and carried the meet of 1921 to its shores.

By-product gas is produced in immense quantities today and is an element of tremendous importance in the industrial life of the community. It is a prime requisite in the successful and economical operation of the steel enterprises, and is indispensable in the operation of the modern furnace. It not only browns the breakfast biscuit, but turns the steel of huge industries to liquid, and makes hot the air that flows into the blast furnace.

The manner in which the gas is captured at a modern furnace plant and is made to serve the stack in which it is created, furnishes an apt illustration of how the iron-making industry has progressed. As the gas forms in the furnace, it is directed into great steel towers, where, roaring like a passing storm, it creates an inferno of heat. The blast of air passes through this white-hot space and reaches the furnace prepared to render maximum efficiency in keeping the furnace hot and making more gas to heat more air to make more gas, while the process of making iron is going forward. This description may seem a bit involved, but the same might be said of the process I have attempted to picture. Running a battery of giant furnaces that are turning out hundreds of tons of iron every few hours is a job that calls for technical skill of the highest order, and a mere layman can form but a crude conception of the way in which the multiplicity of pipes and stacks and whirring engines function. He looks into a tiny opening, like that in a microscope, and sees a seething inferno in the belly of the furnace; his ears are assailed by the roar of burning gas and the thunderous "blow-off" of the hot air as it is released from time to time, and however lucid may be the exposition of how it is all done, the full meaning of some of the scientific terms is bound to be lost. The guide is affable, polite and full of information about heat units, air velocity, chemical content, and the like, and can tell you the revolutions of every hurrying piece of machinery, but what he knows was not acquired in a day, nor can the visitor master it in an hour or two. What the visitor gets is an awe-inspiring sense of the bigness of man's achievements and a new appreciation of the skill and knowledge required in the mastery of the iron industry.

The iron-working industry began in Birmingham on a pretentious scale in 1883, when the first rolling mill was built, going up near the Alice furnace. The enterprise was known as the Birmingham Rolling Mills, and it played a highly important part in the life of the community. For a number of years the prosperity of the city could be accurately gauged by the operations of this plant. When it was going full blast, turning out its maximum capacity of bars, rods and sheet iron, prosperity reigned. When it shut down, a pall of gloom overspread the city and merchants began to cancel orders. However, with the introduction of the steel-producing era, and the erection of the vast chain of enterprises growing out of this development, the old mill became obsolete and finally passed out of existence. Meanwhile the city had grown prodigiously, and the passing of the one-time industrial barometer attracted little attention.

Employing a large number of men when active, this mill became surrounded by quite a large population for that period, and the "Rolling Mill District" was a big factor in politics. The favorite argument used by the candidates who sought to swing the vote was the kind that came in kegs and was delivered through a spigot, with pretzel accompaniments. The position of the aspirant upon the tariff or good roads interested the majority of those lads no whit. Their thirst was not so much for knowledge as for something with a kick.

Several years after the launching of this mill a second enterprise of like character was established at Gate City not far from the site of the old Irondale furnace. It, too, had its day, but finally went the way of the older enterprises, dropping out because it could not keep pace with the quickened industrial life of the district.

CHAPTER XIII

POPULARIZING THE WATER WAGON

WHEN Birmingham first tried the water wagon as a cure for that morning-after sensation, it was only upon the stern insistence of the voters outside the city precincts. Birmingham voted negatively, but the majority in rural Jefferson was sufficient to overcome the urban vote, and the saloons went out amid a pall of gloom. The liquor forces, who long had played a leading, if not a dominant part in the political life of the city, were stunned — but not speechless. Their predictions of disaster were fervid and sincere. They could not conceive of an industrial community surviving a prolonged drouth, and when they closed the swinging doors it was as though they were closing the doors of the city itself.

In the light of what has happened since that first campaign in 1907, it is amusing to recall some of the predictions uttered by men of prominence in the business life of the community. According to these predictions, bats would inhabit the sky-scrapers and grass would grow in the streets. And when these forecasts were made, those essaying the part of a prophet were certain that the bottom was going to drop out. They believed that the workingman had to have his alcoholic stimulant, and were confident that the laboring man would avoid this city. Not only so, but they were convinced that the place would be killed as a trading center, for, they argued, "Who will come to a dry town to buy goods when they could go to another market and get something to drink while supplying their other needs?"

Another prediction was that the city would become bankrupt through loss of revenue following the passing of the saloons and the decreased tax receipts which would attend the wholesale depreciation of property value. The specter of many empty stores added to the feeling of depression and the community braced itself for an era of hard times.

At that period neither state nor national prohibition seemed within the range of probability, and with "wet" cities located in all directions it was thought that Birmingham would become a sort of a plague spot to be avoided by the traveling public as well as the laboring man. What happened was this:

Merchants found that the men who had been spending a large part of their income for drink began to buy more shoes, more clothing and more food for their families, and in a little while all the vacant stores were occupied by new firms, or by old ones that found it necessary to enlarge their business. Instead of empty buildings there arose an almost unprecedented demand for store and office space, and an era of building activity such as the city rarely had witnessed was introduced. Moreover, the laboring man did not resign his job and rush off to a wet town, nor did the city become bankrupt through loss of the saloon license.

It is a remarkable commentary upon these early experiences under prohibition that the loss of revenue occasioned by the passing of the saloon largely was made up through the reduction in expenditures for maintaining peace and order. The police force was cut practically in half and was capable fully to cope with the new conditions.

As shown elsewhere, Birmingham had been a city noted for the frequency with which arguments were settled by the revolver, and it is a matter of record that the great majority of these shooting affrays occurred in saloons. In fact, several saloons were notorious for the number of men who had been killed within their portals, and were pointed out to strangers as the places in which this or that tragedy occurred.

In recalling these days when the wicked crack of the revolver was a common sound and generally was the signal of a funeral, it is astonishing to note the fateful order in which tragedy followed tragedy. There was the case of a fine young fellow (when sober), who stepped into a saloon one night while in a state of intoxication and opened fire at random, killing a man he had never before seen and against whom he could have no grudge. Shortly thereafter the father of this young man, a prominent lawyer, stepped to the cigar counter in the forward part of a saloon and was shot to death by some one who was displaying the exuberance of his feelings by firing a revolver. A little later the son, who had killed a man much as his father was killed, was shot to death in a duel in which his antagonist also was killed, drink being at the bottom of it.

Then there was the case of a young man, the son of one of the pioneer citizens, who had more notches on his gun than I can now recall. He held the record, I believe, for the biggest "bag" in a single night, shooting three men in a saloon row.

Quiet and orderly when sober, his hand instinctively sought the hip-pocket when the liquor began to work. But one evening he drew his weapon on a man who was just as skillful with the revolver, and after a few sharp reports and sudden flashes both men were dead.

Often it happened so, the man who drew the revolver on one occasion falling victim to some other individual who happened to be quick on the trigger and perhaps not quite so much under the influence of the stuff that makes men see red sometimes, and then again makes them see double.

The wanton folly of many of these shooting scrapes was shocking then and is more shocking in the perspective. Men killed because they were drunk and not because they had a grievance. Friends normally, two men would get into an argument over some trivial matter and begin to shoot. If either survived, it was to regret throughout the remainder of life. If neither survived, as happened in a number of cases, it was for widows and orphans to regret.

Several years ago, while riding upon a train in a neighboring state, I happened to say something about Birmingham and a gentleman in the opposite seat remarked, "By Jove, I came near being murdered in that town once." Thereupon he told this story, which further illustrates how the saloon influenced the social order in Birmingham during those wild days:

"I was a stranger in Birmingham and was stopping for the day at a hotel where the bar opened upon the lobby. I walked up to the counter to ask the clerk something when a man I had never before seen leaped upon me and began to slash me with a knife. He acted like a mad-man, cutting furiously, and had slashed me all over the body before I managed to draw my revolver and shoot him. The only thing that saved me was my overcoat. I was laid up in a hospital for a long time, as was my assailant. I had no idea why I had been attacked, and speculated upon the matter no little. Later I learned that the fellow didn't even know me, and had assailed me for no other reason than that he was crazy with drink."

It was thus that the saloon wrote its crimson record in the life of Birmingham, and it was because of these things that the sober and thoughtful citizens of the community decided that it had "sinned away its day of grace," to quote the language of Senator Carmack, the brilliant Tennessean, who was shot to death while fighting the liquor traffic in his own state.

While the vote of citizens in the county outside of Birmingham was necessary to abolish the saloon, it was the women and the ministers of this city who primarily were responsible for the success of the campaign. Their appeals to the balance of the county turned the tide and accomplished the result.

During this heated and spectacular campaign it is said that a party of "workers," representing the "wet" side of the argument, were assigned to cover the northern part of the county. They went forth with literature, cigars and liquid refreshments and presented their cause to all who would listen. About noon one day they came upon a crowd of people who were attending some sort of a benefit dinner out in the woods, the dinner being fifty cents a plate. Here, thought the campaigners, was a golden opportunity. They stirred around among the voters and soon had a large crowd of men eating at their expense. When the feast had been disposed of and the bills had been paid, the workers suggested to the gentlemen who had partaken of their hospitality that they would appreciate their co-operation in the fight against prohibition.

"Well," drawled the self-constituted spokesman of the crowd, "we'd be glad to help you, but seein' as we live in Blount County, we ain't got no right to vote in Jefferson's election."

In their enthusiasm, the campaigners had gone over the county line.

The introduction of prohibition in Birmingham and the remarkable transformation it wrought in this community, had an electrical effect upon the State. The cry arose, "Make Alabama dry," and soon the entire State was engulfed. But success in this, as in many other undertakings, caused another form of intoxication. The prohibition forces, drunk with the unexpected advances, attempted to write prohibition into the constitution of the State, and thereby dug for themselves a pit from which it took several years to climb. Before the amendment election could be held, a reaction had set in, and the measure went down in defeat.

The defeat of the prohibition amendment had the effect of cheering the liquor forces mightily, and they immediately opened a vigorous campaign for the control of the State. Torn by the dissentions which had arisen over the amendment propositiou, the "dry" element failed to present a united front, and the State went back into the "wet" column. But the victory was short-lived. On the next turn-over the prohibitionists won, and Alabama then was placed permanently on the arid list. The long mirrors, the foot-rails and the swinging doors passed from the State to return no more.

Meanwhile the agitation for national prohibition had grown, culminating a few years later in the

HOMES ON THE MOUNTAINSIDE

submission of the constitutional amendment outlawing the traffic in this country.

That the experience of Birmingham under prohibition had a marked effect in bringing about the ratification of the Eighteenth Amendment, undoubtedly is true. As that fight raged inquiries poured into this city from all parts of the country, and frequently visitors came to see for themselves how a large industrial community managed to get along without suds and swinging doors. And what these inquirers found furnished little encouragement to the "wet" forces, for this city thrived amazingly under arid conditions. Here, too, was found a visible and really remarkable illustration of the effect of sobriety — a huge and imposing building that had been transformed from a prison into a parental school.

This jail, erected during the days of the saloon, was designed to care for three hundred prisoners. Built of steel and concrete, and looking not unlike an ancient castle, this building was designed for permanency. No one dreamed that the number of prisoners ever could become so reduced that it would not be needed. Yet this happened. Arrests fell off so rapidly following the abolishment of the saloon, that the old jail, which had become entirely too small while liquor flowed, was ample under the changed conditions. So the fine new jail was closed, and it remained closed for many months. Then the need arose for a school to which unruly children might be sent, and the structure was turned over to the Board of Education.

Pictures of this jail, and the story of its remarkable transition, under the operations of prohibition, were used in newspapers and magazines in many parts of the country, even appearing in some Old World publications as Pussy-foot Johnson proclaimed the dry doctrine to the Britishers.

The reduction in crime and in poverty, and the increase in business and in general efficiency, which attended the final passing of the saloon, were so marked that even the most rabid partisans came to concede the beneficial effects. The majority of citizens in this community had become thoroughly reconciled to their ration of water or "soft" drinks long before the Nation decided that it could get along without that morning-after feeling.

As a matter of course, prohibition, City, State or National, did not stop the sale and consumption of liquors in their entirety. The boot-leggers and the moonshiners appeared on the scene when the saloon went, and they continue to ply a hazardous trade, but the amount of liquor consumed is infinitesimal compared with the quantity used in the old days. One may observe the crowds that throng the streets day after day, and only once in a long, long time will he see a person whose feet have lost the sense of direction. This is due to several causes, chief among them being the fact that the great majority of men who once drank openly in saloons, and sometimes to excess, have found that they are better off without it, or will not take the trouble to hunt out blind-tiger liquor. Then those who want it and are willing to go to some trouble to get it, are afraid of the stuff handed them in exchange for their money. Wood alcohol has gotten in its deadly work here as elsewhere, and the result has been to inspire a wholesome dread of liquors the genesis of which is in doubt. Here the man who complained bitterly about being the victim of an accident and, upon being asked for particulars, said "A friend asked me to have a drink and I didn't hear him," might well be congratulated, for one never knows what he is getting. It may be something with a "kick," and then again it may be something with slow music and flowers.

After voting against prohibition in the first campaign, Birmingham voted in favor of it when the final overthrow came, thus giving concrete evidence of its changed opinion about the value of the saloon, as a community builder.

Another striking illustration of the changed sentiment of the city upon issues having a moral or religious significance, is found in the attitude of the people toward Sunday observance. This city once had open theatres on Sunday, but these places of amusement were closed by a vote of the people. And a rather remarkable thing developed in this election. The exponents of the Sunday theatre insisted that the workingman should have an opportunity to find amusement on his day of rest. It was argued that the rich man had his golf, or his automobile, with which to enjoy recreation, but that the workingman had no such avenues of entertainment, and should be allowed to enjoy a show with his family. When the returns were in it developed that the boxes where the labor vote was strongest gave the heaviest majorities against the opening of theatres on Sunday.

Sunday baseball also is banned in Birmingham, so far as professional contests go, yet it is the best baseball town in the Southern League. Year after year, Birmingham leads the South in point of attendance, a condition which is eminently satisfactory to the management, and which must suit the "fans" because there has been no outspoken demand for Sunday ball. The average man figures that he can get off for an afternoon during the week and reserve his Sunday for something else, whereas with Sunday ball he might not be able to get that afternoon off.

This sentiment for prohibition, for law enforcement and for Sabbath observance, is not an accidental growth, but is the by-product of zealous effort on the part of that element which is responsible for Birmingham's record-breaking Sunday School classes, for its strong laymen's associations, and for its exceptionally large church attendance. In brief, it all harks back to the preachers. They have, by united effort, succeeded in making the church as powerful as the saloon used to be.

The term "united effort" is used advisedly, because the preaching fraternity has a union all its own, and when this organization gets behind a movement of any kind, the chances are that it will triumph.

One of the dominant figures in the pastors' union is Dr. George R. Stuart, who for years united with that famous and spectacular evangelist, Sam Jones, in flaying the devil from one end of the country to the other. Pastor of the largest church in the city, and speaking at every service to a crowd that taxes the capacity of the house, Dr. Stuart makes a dent in any situation he attacks, and when the same cause he is espousing is being espoused from a hundred other pulpits, something always happens.

Another preacher, not so picturesque as Dr. Stuart, but an organizer of exceptional ability, is Dr. J. M. Broady, pastor of the one great Presbyterian church in Birmingham that is "Northern" instead of "Southern." An athlete, an accomplished horseman, and a fighter from the cow country of the West, he, too, is a power when it comes to a campaign for the things the church stands for. And there are others, plenty of them, who do not hesitate to jump into a fight, when to jump seems the proper thing.

These preachers, with melancholy memories of things as they used to be, and of the long and bitter campaigns through which they went in order to bring about improved conditions, are fixed in their purpose not to permit any backsliding. As a consequence, the so-called wide-open element is ever chary about attempting to put anything over.

Perhaps one of the reasons why Birmingham citizens are so strong in their support of the preachers, is because they will not have any but the best pulpit material. Competition between the big churches is as strong as that existing between rival business houses, and all of them insist upon having the biggest men available. The Methodists, the Baptists and the Presbyterians represent the churches which lead in membership, and the achievement of one is a constant challenge to the others. The rivalry is friendly but real, and the co-operation is perfect.

A rather striking illustration of the popular attitude toward the preacher, was given less than a year ago, when a loving cup was offered to the person rendering the most distinguished service to the community during the preceding twelve months. The award was made by a committee representing all the civic organizations of the city, and the cup went to a Presbyterian preacher, Rev. J. A. Bryan, by a unanimous vote. Many citizens who had achieved large things along material lines were put in nomination, but the overwhelming sentiment throughout the community was in favor of giving it to this humble pastor of one of the smaller churches. Thousands of people attended the presentation ceremonies, and no man ever received a greater ovation than was given this lank and lovable minister.

Rev. Bryan is a unique figure in the religious life of the city. He has lived here, serving the one church for more than thirty-five years, and about the first thing a grief-stricken family thinks of doing is sending for "Brother Bryan," this regardless of denominational affiliations. It is doubtful if any man living has conducted more funerals or brought solace to more men and women and children in their hours of grief.

Until his death a dozen years ago, Birmingham had in Dr. Luman S. Handley, another minister who filled a similar place in the life of the community. An ex-Confederate soldier, Dr. Handley came here when the town was little more than a mud hole, and he literally loved his way into the hearts of the people through nearly forty years of service. More than any one else, he kindled the fires of fraternalism between denominations, and made possible the fine spirit of friendship and esteem which exists between these denominations today. When his congregation was without a church home at one time, the leading Jewish congregation of the city tendered him the use of their synagogue, and for over a year Christ was preached in this temple. Later, when the thirty-fifth anniversary of Dr. Handley's pastorate was celebrated, he was presented with a beautiful loving cup by the members of this Synagogue, the Temple Emanu-el.

That this fine spirit existed between other congregations was shown when this same body of Jewish churchmen were temporarily without a place of worship, pending the completion of a new temple. Baptists, Presbyterians and others offered the use of their churches, and one of these tenders was accepted.

When Dr. Handley was presented with the loving cup, he told a number of stories about the early days of Birmingham, one of which concerned the marriage of a young foreigner. "After the ceremony," said Dr. Handley, "the young fellow called me to one side, and, slipping a silver dollar in my hand, whispered, 'This is all I can afford now, Doctor, but I will try to do better next time!' "

Full of the grace of God, this good man died, his memory being perpetuated by the Handley Memorial Presbyterian Church.

Today one of the oldest ministers, in point of service, is Rabbi Morris Newfield, of Temple Emanu-el, whose learning was recognized by the Baptists in his election to the faculty of their college in this city.

Another outstanding figure is "Parson" Barnwell, Rector of the Church of the Advent, the leading Episcopal Church of the city, and the one formerly served by Dr. Murray, now Bishop of Maryland. A brilliant speaker and a great "mixer," Dr. Barnwell has a strong hold upon the young men of the city. A similar position is occupied by Dr. Henry M. Edmonds, pastor of the Independent Presbyterian Church, and one of the best known pulpit orators in the South. Dr. John A. MacSporran, pastor of the First Presbyterian Church, is another "young man's man," and Dr. James E. Dillard, of the Southside Baptist Church, may be placed in the same category. A young man's town, Birmingham, in selecting ministers, calls for men who can meet the spirit of youth upon familiar terms.

CHAPTER XIV

THE SWAY OF KING COTTON

AS gold suggests to the Californian the tragedy and romance of other days, so cotton stirs the imagination of the Southerner, and conjures up pictures of vanished years; pictures of big white houses, adorned with stately columns, and surrounded by far-reaching fields of white; of low-roofed cabins, where dark-hued children play, and where, when the moon rides high, the plaintive voice of the negro is heard, keeping time to the banjo or guitar; pictures of river boats, their decks piled high with bales and their smoke-stacks belching fire as they race for New Orleans; pictures of fleet and shining horses thundering down the final stretch; pictures of ancient triumphs, and pictures of vanished glories. And, thinking of these things, the old-time Southerner knows what was in the heart of the poet when he said:

> "Tears, idle tears, I know not what they mean.
> Tears from the depth of some divine despair
> Rise in the heart, and gather to the eyes,
> In looking on the happy Autumn-fields,
> And thinking of the days that are no more."

For generations cotton was the main-stay of the South, and today it constitutes the greatest single item in its economic life. Crop diversification has come, manufacturing interests have attained huge proportions, and the development of mineral resources has brought wealth beyond anything dreamed of in the olden days, but cotton continues to be a mighty factor in the lives of the people, and time will not change this condition. Nor is it surprising that this should be so, for cotton is not only one of the most wonderful prodncts of nature, but it is well-nigh indispensable. It played a part in the lives of old-world peoples before the coming of Christ, and from century to century furnished the attire of multitudes. Herodotus referred to its growth in India, Pliny spoke of it as an Egyptian product, Cortez was presented with gifts of cotton fabric in Mexico four hundred years ago, and Columbus found it growing wild when he discovered America. So, an ancient and honorable plant, it has its place both in the history of past years and the every-day life of the present.

While little of this staple is produced in the rugged hills about Birmingham where are deposited the minerals upon which the wealth of this city is based, cotton is an important factor in the industrial life of the community. In Birmingham it is the basis of an industry that extends to every spot on the globe where sunshine and soil tempt the blossom into bloom.

Birmingham is the home of the greatest cotton gin manufacturing enterprise in the world, and from these factories cotton working machinery goes to South and Central America, to Africa, to Russia, to Turkey and Persia, to China and the Philippines, and wherever else the snowy staple rears its head.

What the development of the perfecting press and the typesetting machine were to the printing profession, the development of the gin was to the cotton industry. Until that shrewd Yankee, Eli Whitney, visited Georgia in 1792 and there received the inspiration which led to the invention of the gin, the separation of short lint cotton from the seed was a slow and tedious process, performed by hand. Without slave labor, the cost would have been prohibitive, and even with this labor, the time consumed was so great that production was held to an abnormally low figure. Whitney's gin, the patent for which was issued in 1794 and was signed by George Washington, gave a tremendous impetus to the growth of cotton, and as improvements were introduced, the production grew until the number of bales were counted in millions instead of in thousands.

Whitney was a native of Massachusetts, and it is a rather remarkable fact that he and another New Englander, Daniel Pratt, should have played so large a part in the development of a Southern industry. The latter, a native of New Hampshire, came to Alabama in 1832, and several years later began the manufacture of gins in a little plant which he built upon a creek where Prattville stands today. The Pratt gin embodied many improvements, and when the plant was taken over by the Continental Gin Company of Birmingham, it was the largest producer in the United States.

Birmingham's connection with the industry began late, but because of revolutionary inventions put into operation here, this soon became the center of activities, the Birmingham concern absorbing existing establishments in many parts of the country. This rise of leadership in the manufacturing of gins began with the invention in Texas of a pneumatic cotton elevator, the designer being R. S. Munger. By means of this invention the cotton was taken direct from the wagon to the gin and upon passing through the gin (being thoroughly cleaned in the process), was carried direct to the press. This method saved an infinite amount of labor and time, and in a few years those who controlled the invention controlled the cotton gin industry to a very large extent. Because of the proximity of the raw material for manufacturing the gins, the industry was brought to Birmingham, where it grew with prodigious rapidity. Whitney and Pratt, the New Englanders, made gins that were effective in separating the lint from the seed. Munger, the Southerner, made a gin that sucked the seed cotton from the wagon and delivered a bale of cotton pressed, cleaned and wrapped, all the labor once performed by hand being performed by the machine, and at an almost inconceivable speed.

Cotton constitutes a really wonderful plant, and because it is one of the cheapest products on earth, the variety of uses to which it is put is multiplying rapidly. The blossoms, stretching for miles upon the big plantations, furnish the bee with the nector from which is produced the most delicious honey known to the breakfast table. The fiber enters into the making of millions of yards of undisguised cotton goods, and is the chief element in other millions of yards of lustrous goods, beautifully disguised as silk. Its uses in the industrial field range all the way from the making of car wheels to the production of high explosives.

For many years the seed of the cotton seemed worthless except for purposes of reproduction, and if the value of the seed thrown away could be recovered today it would pay the national debt. This dark and fuzzy little seed furnishes meal for livestock and bread for man. Its oil fits in beautifully for all the purposes to which olive oil is adapted, and in many instances olive oil has been pushed aside by this new and wonderful by-product. It is used for salad dressing and enters into the making of the most delectable cakes and pies. The cotton seed produces butter that claims no kinship with the cow and lard that is not remotely related to the hog. Not only so, but it invades other fields than that of food supply, and appears in the form of soap and paint and grease.

The branch of the cotton industry opened through the discovery that the seed contained many wonderful properties, though comparatively new, has attained enormous proportions. Moreover, new refinements are being discovered constantly, and today the lowly cotton seed has won a measure of esteem quite equal to that accorded the fiber itself.

While cotton constitutes one of the world's

greatest necessities, and fulfills many imperative needs, its production is perhaps the biggest gamble in the agricultural game. The grower must fight the boll weevil and the grass during the months that the crop is maturing, and, if he is fortunate enough to get a good crop to market, he then must stand off and watch the bulls and bears fight over the price he is to receive. The variations in price are astonishing, and fill the heart of the producer with alternate hope and despair. During the war cotton sold for over forty cents a pound. Today it is around ten cents a pound, and many growers and dealers in the South have war-time cotton on their hands, upon which they borrowed more than the staple will bring at this time. It has been estimated by a careful student of the subject that if cotton were produced under the same conditions that exist in the industrial field, the cost would be one dollar a pound. But the eight-hour day, with time-and-a-half for overtime, has not been introduced upon the Southern plantation, and the world continues to find its greatest bargains at the cotton counter.

The manufacture of cotton goods and cotton seed products constitutes a huge industry in Birmingham, and it seems more than passing strange that two such universally adaptable products as cotton and coal should abound in the same territory; coal with its infinite variety of by-products, ranging from gas, oil and acids to perfumes and medicines, and cotton, which makes possible ragless paper, cocoonless silk, creamless ice cream, hogless lard and wheatless bread.

The once lowly peanut also has an active part in the industrial life of Birmingham, having graduated from circus adjunct, and boon companion to red lemonade, into an article of commerce that is of great importance. Alabama leads the world in the production of peanuts, having attained this distinction while fighting the inroads of the boll weevil with the weapon of diversification. Until the coming of the cotton pest, the peanut was regarded generally as a convenient something upon which to clamp the jaws while watching the death-defying leaps of the trapeze performers, or to slip to the baby elephants in passing through the animal tent, but its place in the industrial world was just about nil.

At this stage entered Mr. Boll Weevil, the blight of his presence being felt throughout the far-flung cotton belt. In Alabama the Department of Agriculture began a frantic search for things that Alabama farmers grow in lieu of cotton, and one of the results was the peanut. Experiments proved that salad oils, butter, lard, soap, paint, nitro-glycerine and other valuable products could

WORLD'S LARGEST ROTARY COAL DUMP

WORLD'S LARGEST LAKE OF PITCH

be extracted from the peanut, and Alabama turned to its production with an enthusiasm that was eloquent of its desire for relief from the cotton situation. At the same time mills for the extraction of the hidden properties of the peanut sprang up in many parts of the state, and there was laid the foundation of a new form of agricultural and industrial activity.

As an evidence of appreciation for what the boll weevil did in driving the farmers of Alabama to the raising of peanuts, velvet beans, tobacco, alfalfa and similar products, the people of South Alabama erected a monument to that energetic bug, the testimonial being unveiled several years ago with elaborate ceremonies.

While truck farming constitutes an important factor in the territory adjacent to Birmingham, the real agricultural life of the State centers in a territory located south of this city, known as the "Black Belt." This name is not given as indicative of the color of the population, although the negroes are largely in the majority, but is derived from the color of the soil.

The "Black Belt," which has an average width of about eighteen miles, traverses the State a little south of the center, and ends just across the Mississippi line. Though it is hundreds of miles from salt water, there is evidence that the "Black Belt" once formed the bottom of a great sea. Petrified fish bones, sea shells and similar evidence of prehistoric life abound, and the soil is said by experts to be as rich as any found upon this continent. Even in anti-bellum days, when communication was slow and travel was fraught with great difficulty, the fame of the "Black Belt" was widespread, and much Eastern capital found its way into the territory. As much as $100 per acre was paid for the land back in those days; this at a time when ordinary lands could be purchased for a dollar an acre. However, the advent of war, culminated in the passing of slave labor, wrought a mighty change in this prosperous section. Land values dropped as much as ninety percent in many instances, and, in lieu of slave labor, came the tenant system—owners renting out broad and fertile acres to ex-slaves, usually upon a basis of one-half the total crop. The owner of the land supplied the things needful for production of the crops, including animals, implements, seeds, etc., and also furnished the necessities of life to the tenant and his family.

When the crops were garnered, would come the settlement between the owner and tenant. The value of the products was ascertained, and fifty percent of the whole was credited to the landowner and fifty percent to the tenant. Then from the tenant's half was deducted the amount charged against him for supplies. This system, practiced with honesty as between the conscientious land owner and the ignorant black, worked in an equitable and satisfactory manner, but, as might have been expected, the time came when the land fell into the hands of some who had no scruples about dealing with the negro, and out of this condition grew a long chain of abuses. The "advance merchant" came upon the scene, removing from the shoulders of the land owner the burden of providing the tenant with the things needful for producing the crop and maintaining his family between seasons.

Many of these merchants played a useful and constructive part in keeping the agriculture of the South moving, but, as always under such circumstances, the man looking for a big profit, and having no compunctions as to how it was obtained, found this a lucrative field. The schemes to which he would resort in robbing the negro of the fruit of his toil is the theme of many a story, and they illustrate a genius for wrongdoing, as well as a surprising indifference to the Golden Rule. One of the common practices of this element is said to have been to start a "charge column" with the year, then add the purchases from time to time, thus:

Bought:	Sept. 1, 1868
1 sack of meal..........	$2.40
1 pr. shoes..............	3.00
10 lbs. coffee............	1.50

When the time of settlement came, the year went into the total charged against the farmer, along with such other extraordinary charges as might have suggested themselves during the twelve months, and he was a lucky individual who had anything left after the settlement.

The impression made upon the mind of the negro tenant by practices of this kind, was well illustrated on one occasion when a wealthy citizen from the North came into Alabama with a view to buying a large plantation which had been offered for sale. The deal was considered so important that the real estate man handling the matter called upon the Agricultural Department of the State for the assistance of an expert in explaining the nature of the soil and the wide variety of products to which it was adapted. The visitor was much impressed and was about to close the deal when he fell into conversation with an aged darky, and then it looked for a few minutes as though the real estate man might lose a fat commission and the State a new citizen.

While the parties to the transaction were seated

upon the broad veranda of the old mansion which adorned this plantation, the prospective buyer observed an aged negro seated by an overflowing artesian well that bubbled up near the house, and he strolled over to the darky, whereupon the following conversation was overheard by the real estate dealer and the agent from the Agricultural Department:

"How long have you lived here?" asked the prospective buyer.

"All my life, Boss; I was borned on this here place befo' de wah, an' when de niggers was freed I stayed on here," was the reply of the darky.

"Then you know this plantation very well?"

"I does dat; I knows every foot of it, an' I knows it am de best place in dis whole country. I knows mo' cawn an' cotton is hauled off'n dis place ever year dan off'm nair uther place hereabout."

At this the prospective buyer smiled his appreciation, and the real estate man whispered "that ought to cinch matters," but the conversation at the well was not over, for the gentleman continued:

"Then I ought to make a lot of money off of this plantation, eh?"

"No, sah, Boss, you can't make no money. If you does it'll be the fust time anybody ever done it since de wah."

The jaw of the Northerner sagged and he gasped:

"If it's such fine land and produces such splendid crops, why is it money cannot be made here?"

"Well, Boss, to tell you de truf, de ducks eats it all up; yes sah, de ducks takes it all!"

"The ducks eat it up! What on earth do you mean by that?"

"Yes, sir, de ducks eats it up, just like I's tellin' you. We niggers raises heaps of cotton an' heaps of cawn, an' den we takes it to town to de sto'. Den de white folks dey figgers an' figgers, an' dey ducks dis and dey ducks dat, and 'fo de Lawd, by time dey's done, de ducks is et up ever' thing we's raised!"

When the Northerner realized that the darky's reference to "de ducks" meant "deducts," he was vastly amused and exacted from the aged negro a promise that he would remain on the place after he purchased it, assuring him that "de ducks" wouldn't hamper the operation of the plantation in the future.

Today the old-time advance merchant largely is a creature of the past, education and diversification having proved his undoing. Many farmers are able to finance their own operations, and those who cannot have the help of the banker or the legitimate merchant. So "de ducks" are not so destructive of farm values as they were in olden times.

South of the far-famed "Black Belt" there is a rich and fertile section where the products cover a wide range, including numerous varieties of fruit, berries, melons and nuts. Similar conditions exist in the farming section throughout upper Alabama, though in this part of the State semi-tropical fruits and choicer garden products do not flourish as prodigiously, nor mature so early in the year.

Were it without mineral deposits of any character, Alabama still would be a rich State because of the abundance of its agricultural output and the wide variety of products its equitable climate makes possible. In view of this fact, Birmingham might aptly be termed an island of industry completely surrounded by a sea of agricultural activity, and this condition simplifies the problem of what to eat and where to get it. Vegetables and fruits of almost every variety are obtainable within a few hours after they are gathered. And so with sea foods. Fish, crabs, shrimp, etc., brought into Mobile harbor this evening may be served upon the table of the Birmingham citizen tomorrow morning, together with grapefruit, oranges, strawberries, cantaloupes or figs that are plucked today. The problem of something to put in the morning coffee, or to serve with the breakfast cereal, is simplified by the fact that there are approximately one hundred and fifty dairies within twenty miles of the city.

CHAPTER XV

BLAZING NEW TRAILS

OWING to the unusual character of the materials with which they had to work, creative effort of the highest order was necessary on the part of those who blazed the way for industry in this district, and lent wings to its hesitant feet.

The utmost ingenuity was required in the development of processes for the successful and economical production of iron and steel, the experiments which finally were crowned with success, extending over a number of years, and the results being a complete surprise to the world's chief authorities in metallurgical matters.

This early call for resourcefulness in dealing with new and unexplored fields, if those fields were to become productive, had the effect of developing a school of thinkers, out of whose researches have come many contributions to industrial progress.

To make practical and profitable the use of materials which seemed impossible of utilization in competition with established industries, following established practices with materials whose secrets were mastered long since, was to put Birmingham upon a sound and permanent basis. The inventions by means of which this was aecomplished were followed by many others that gave to permanency the elements of speed and safety.

Processes invented in Birmingham in the beginning had to do with local materials and were not always susceptible of general adaptation. Not so with many of those which subsequently came out of that hard school of exploration into the unknown. Many mechanical inventions and chemical processes evolved here have found nation-wide application.

In the mining of bituminous coal, which is highly productive of explosive material, tremendous advances have been made, with the result that mine disasters have become exceedingly rare. Indeed, the complete story of what has been accomplished in promoting safety in mines and mills and factories in the Birmingham district would make a volume in itself, and would bear eloquent testimony to the inventive genius of those behind the great industrial agencies of the district.

A rather remarkable thing in connection with Birmingham inventions is that when one undertakes to trace many of them to their origin, the trail leads right up to the desk of some millionaire; some big industrial figure, whose incentive was not the money that might be obtained through a successful patent, but was the result of a keen desire to accomplish better things than were being accomplished under the existing order.

These heads of huge enterprises became inventors because they wanted to see ends attained with greater speed; because they wanted to simplify processes and eliminate lost motion, and because they wanted to see results standardized. If they saw an opportunity to plant a machine that would make two men go, where they had to use four under old conditions, they applied themselves to the task and usually accomplished what they went after.

There is nothing about these inventions that suggests the long-haired theorist, hopeful of perfecting a perpetual motion machine, and thereby becoming wealthy beyond the dreams of avarice. Hard-headed and dynamic individuals, determined to make their particular mine, furnace or mill more effective than the mine or furnace or mill of the other fellow, they have evolved their process and their machines for the joy of seeing ends accomplished more effectually and more expeditiously.

As a rule the two-fold purpose behind these displays of inventive genius has been, first, to insure greater safety, and, second, to minimize cost through the elimination of labor.

An apt illustration of this two-fold idea is found in the invention of the Ramsay Rotary dump, conceived over twenty years ago by Erskine Ramsay with a view to meeting a local situation, but since adopted by industrial organizations throughout the country, many of the appliances being in use in the great coal fields of Pennsylvania.

Mr. Ramsay, now a millionaire coal operator, conceived the idea that if the cars composing a train could be dumped one at a time, or in multiple, many improvements and economies in mining practices would result. Chief among these advantages would be the elimination of end gates and drop-bottoms in mine cars, and the ability to handle an entire train of as many as thirty cars, as is now being done, without uncoupling the train from the haulage rope, or motor, or the cars from each other. The elimination of the doors was to prevent the escape of coal, which under the old system filled the mine entries and haulage roads with the fine dust that is one of the chief causes of mine explosions.

The first of these dumps was installed at an ore mine on Red Mountain by the Tennessee Company. Today they are in use, not only at ore and coal mines throughout the country, but have been adapted to the handling of sugar beets, phosphate rock and salt. The largest plant of the kind in the world was manufactured for and is now in use by the Snowden Coke Company near Pittsburgh. It receives and dumps a trip of twenty-eight mine cars, emptying them in ten seconds.

Prior to the development of a process for the manufacture of steel from Birmingham iron, work of the highest importance was performed by Mr. Ramsay in developing processes for improving the quality of the raw materials. While he was Chief Engineer of the Tennessee Company, before it was taken over by the Steel Corporation, he developed an improved coal washer that was adopted by numerous producers. From washing no coal at all, the Tennessee Company began washing every pound that it put into coke, and the improvement in quality formed an important contribution to the successful conversion of Alabama iron into basic open hearth steel.

The Ramsay coal sampler is another invention to the credit of this engineer. It takes samples from a large proportion of the coal mined during the day, and the operator is enabled to learn just the quality of the coal each miner is loading. The result is a cleaner coal. Mr. Ramsay also built, in the Birmingham shop, the first shaking screen for bituminous coal manufactured in the United States, and he followed this with the invention of a feeder, now in use in many plants throughout the country. Mine cars, car wheels and bearings also commanded his attention, with the result that he has practically covered the entire mining field, including coke ovens and furnaces. The list includes an overhead, slow-moving, rope haulage system, which has been installed in Alabama, and is now being put in service at the mines of the Tennessee Consolidated Coal Company in Tennessee.

The same problem which Erskine Ramsay solved with his early invention was solved by another Birmingham engineer, Edwin J. Best, with an automatic rotary dump, the power for which is furnished by the car itself. The unbalanced weight of the loaded car causes the dump to turn over, and as it turns it develops sufficient power, through a fly-wheel, to enable the empty car to return to its normal position. This ingenious contrivance eliminates the necessity of a power drive, and is another conservator of labor.

Another important invention by another man whose genius has been applied because problems had to be solved, and not because of any idea of making money out of a patent, is a tunnel system of handling and distributing the elements entering into the making of iron. Under this system, the car in which the various ingredients are assembled is run through a tunnel, above which are stored the various grades of ore, the coke, the limestone, and the dolomite. As the car advances, these materials are fed into it automatically, each in the proper proportion, and when the car is filled its contents is conveyed by a skip-hoist to the top of the furnace, where it is dumped into the hot and hungry interior.

This system is the invention of "Rick" Woodward, the head of one of the greatest industrial organizations in the district, and also the owner of Birmingham's baseball park and franchise. The son of J. H. Woodward, one of the pioneer developers of Alabama, and a man who believed that boys should start at the bottom, Rick Woodward learned to be an engineer under the urging of his millionaire father. During the recent strike on the Atlanta, Birmingham & Atlantic Railroad, when the whole system was tied up, he put on overalls, climbed into the cab of a locomotive, and pulled a train over the road until other help could be obtained. A director in this railroad, he climbed back in the cab, after years of absence, because he didn't like to see the wheels standing still. Later he was much surprised when the newspapers over the country came out with first-page headlines reading "Millionaire Engineer Pulls Train When Men Strike," and by the picturesque stories that followed.

Another leading figure in the industrial field who has been tireless in the development of new processes and refinements is George Gordon Crawford, president of most of the subsidiary organizations of the United States Steel Corporation in Alabama. His contributions to the steel and iron industry have been invaluable, and he is also the inventor of a water seal for gas mains which has supplanted the ordinary type of valve all over the world.

Furnaces are connected up by immense gas pipes, and when one of a battery has to be shut down for repairs the connecting pipe must be closed to shut off the gas. The old method was to use a metal valve which nearly always became leaky through infrequent use, and it happened on numerous occasions that walls of brick had to be built in the pipe to effect a seal. The water seal made it possible to shut off the gas in less than a minute, and keep it shut off absolutely, the process involving nothing more than turning a cock. To open the valve when repairs were completed was equally simple. This tremendously important invention, devised to meet a local situation and with no idea of its value as a patented device, caught the attention of one of the big national figures in the ironmaking industry and was patented at his suggestion. Since then it has become of universal application.

A Birmingham inventor whose genius has resulted in the establishment of a national industry of world-wide significance is R. S. Munger, whose organization has plants scattered from Texas to Massachusetts. His inventions, numbering scores, relate to cotton handling equipment.

To a Birmingham inventor also is due the credit for another basic patent which has become the foundation of a vast industry—the steam turbine. Some twenty years ago, James Wilkinson, an engineer in the employ of the local street railway company, developed nearly a hundred inventions relating to the turbine, which had just begun to attract the attention of engineers. With practically no capital and very little encouragement, Wilkinson built three steam turbines, two of which were sold to the New York Central Railroad Company and installed in a pumping plant near Albany, N. Y. The success of the engines brought local capitalists to the assistance of the inventor. Later, when the attention of the outside world had been attracted and bidding for the Wilkinson patents became spirited, all those having stock in the enterprise expected to reap pounds where they had sown pennies. For a time it seemed as if they would, too, but the big agencies which sought control of the patents were shrewd enough to get together when it came to buying. Thus, while a substantial sum was received the dreams of a lot of stockholders that they would become rich over night were not realized. Ultimately the patents became the property of the General Electric Company and proved an important element in engineering progress.

The mail cranes which stand on the right-of-way of practically all Southern railroads and from which passing trains snatch bags laden with bills, billet-doux and the like is the invention of a Birmingham man, W. S. Davidson.

An invention that grew out of inability to find enough giants to perform what used to be the most back-breaking labor about furnaces was produced by J. P. Dovel, an engineer of the Sloss Company, in a "pig breaker" that is now used generally. In the old days it was almost impossible for furnace companies to keep enough men who had the strength necessary to "break pig," a task which consisted in breaking up the pieces of iron that are formed every time the molten metal is run into the molding beds.

The "bed" in which pig iron is cast at the average furnace is made of sand, filled with half-moon depressions. All of these minor depressions, which form the "pig" or iron slab, are joined together by a slightly larger depression which forms a "ditch" through which the molten iron runs in reaching the minor depressions. A rough idea of what I am attempting to describe may be obtained by imagining the form that would be left were a coarse comb pressed into a flat piece of dough. The back of the comb would make the trough through which the molten metal flows, while the teeth would form the depressions into which the iron flows off to become "pig." It was in breaking this long piece of iron up into small lengths, like the "pig," and in breaking the "pig" from the "back" of the comb that such tremendous energy was wasted in the old days. Giant negroes usually performed the task, and it was slow and exhausting work. The machine invented by Dovel seizes these heavy pieces of iron and breaks them up as though they were so many matches. Thus ended the quest for giants.

While not so spectacular as the inventions produced in the mechanical world, the inventions coming from the laboratories of the Birmingham district have been quite as important. They made possible the remarkable results obtained in producing steel from the low-grade ores which abound in North Alabama, and, naturally, the chemical engineers take great pride in the results that have been attained. What they have accomplished was again and again declared to be impossible.

An exception to the general run of Birmingham inventors was Andrew Jackson Beard, an old-time darky, whose mechanical conceptions caused many local citizens to contribute sundry sums of money and to dream dreams of future wealth.

Andy was a typical ante-bellum negro, but one gifted with exceptional ingenuity. Able neither to read nor to write, and without any mechanical training, he evolved a number of devices that for a time promised to produce revolutionary results. One of these contrivances was a car coupler, and when he displayed it at a convention of the Master Car Builders' Association in Atlantic City some years ago it made such an impression that Andy was elected an honorary member of the organization. An humble and unpretentious darky, he cherished the memory of his Atlantic City experience so long as he lived and counted his election as an honorary member of the Master Car Builders' Association as one of the greatest distinctions that could come to man. Until his death he continued assiduously to work upon his invention, hoping always to perfect it and to see it universally adopted as a standard. Among many other white men who assisted Andy from time to time and tried to make his dream come true was W. Melville Drennen, wealthy merchant and twice mayor of Birmingham.

Though riches never rewarded the patient endeavors of this unique darky, the interest taken in him and his work by white friends was such that he lived comfortably and was able to spend his days in hope, the rainbow tints of which were not darkened by the shadows of want.

In recalling this darky and his inventions, I am reminded that the idea that a negro was worth insuring originated in Birmingham, and that out of the practical application of this idea developed a business that runs into the millions. A number of years ago a local citizen who owned a large plantation in another part of the State suffered heavy losses because of an epidemic of some kind that took off several of his negro "hands" just when their services were needed to care for crops that were ready for harvest. The losses consequent upon inability to get other help suggested the idea of insuring the lives of such employees, but when the matter was gone into it was found that standard insurance companies did not accept such risks. Thereupon an insurance company designed especially for the protection of negroes was organized. It developed into quite a success, and then others were formed along the same lines. Later many standard companies of the old school let down the bars to the physically sound among the black race with the result that today the darky has no difficulty in obtaining insurance. In fact, he has considerable difficulty in avoiding it if he lives in a city, for some of these companies have a weekly pay system with many live and skillful agents in the field.

Following the development of the life insurance idea, as applied to the negro, came the "sick benefit" and the "funeral benefit," both of which found an almost instant response among darkies. Incidentally it may be observed that this "sick benefit" shares with the hookworm and the malarial mosquito such credit as is due for the prevalence of ills among the blacks of the South.

As with white physicians, it is not always possible for the colored practitioner to determine the nature of the ill with which the patient is afflicted, and the patient frequently is unable to give him any information other than he has a "misery" in the back or an "ailin'" in the side. Just how to diagnose a case when the truth was in doubt remained a puzzling problem until some court rendered a decision holding that one having a sick-benefit policy might recover when ill from malaria. This decision simplified matters immensely, though the sudden increase in malaria in various Southern cities was not so complimentary to the efficiency of health authorities as to the perception of certain physicians. Still, it enabled patients to collect sick benefits and, collecting sick benefits, they were in position to pay promptly for professional attention, which seems to justify the adage that it's an ill wind that blows nobody a kiss.

CHAPTER XVI

REFORMING THE PUBLIC DOLLAR

THE story of the simple-minded flood victim who sought assistance from the mayor is told frequently as an illustration of the way in which municipal officials function, and the gusto with which it is related furnishes an example of the all-too-prevalent attitude toward the government which comes closest to the people and which should be most responsive to their needs.

According to this story, a man residing in a low section of a mid-western city suffered the loss of all his chickens when the neighborhood was swept by a flood. Someone to whom he was pouring out his tale of woe suggested that he call upon the mayor for relief. A few days later the man making the suggestion met the unfortunate chicken fancier and the following dialogue took place:

"Did you go to the mayor about your chickens being drowned?"

"Yes, I went right away."

"Well, did he give you any money?"

"No, but he was free with his advice — told me to cut out the chickens and raise ducks."

At this juncture everybody is supposed to laugh, the point being that a man should have more sense than to expect something from his government. Undoubtedly, there is a disposition on the part of many city dwellers to expect a very small return upon the money they invest in their local government. Their idea seems to be that the public till has a most demoralizing effect upon coin and currency; that however sober and industrious a dollar may have been while at work in the channels of trade or commerce it quits the path of rectitude upon falling under the spell of the public treasury and henceforth is a profligate.

To give this profligate public dollar a purchasing power equal to that possessed by the thrifty private dollar has been the dream of many, and numerous instances are on record where gratifying results were obtained, but there is enough waste in American cities today to keep alive the feeling that the public dollar is dissolute beyond redemption; that in spite of all that is said and done it will continue to go the way of the wanton.

As a consequence of repeated failures at reform a spirit of cynicism has been developed that has proved a very wall of obstruction in many communities. This spirit finds expression on the one hand in blind indifference to governmental matters, while on the other hand it is manifested in an attitude of destructive criticism: nothing is done right, nothing can be done right, therefore nothing should be attempted.

Any development, the tendency of which is to alter this attitude of indifference and to eliminate doubt respecting the possibility of sane and constructive accomplishments through governmental agencies would appear to be worthy of consideration. In this connection some encouragement may be found in Birmingham's experience during the three years of mounting prices and growing demands incident to the World War. The city came through this period of extraordinary stress with a balance on the right side of the ledger; a practical illustration of the fact that the public dollar may be reformed and an actual demonstration of efficiency that should furnish a ray of hope to the political dyspeptic who has ceased to believe that anything can come out of municipal government that does not cost more than it should.

The experience of this city during the three war years is portrayed in the following figures:

In 1918 the cost of operation was $42,092.11 under the receipts; in 1919 the excess of receipts over expenditures for current expenses was $130,-905.24; in 1920 the difference on the right side of the ledger was $40,588.46. This result was achieved not by a quintet of financial wizards, but by a board consisting of Dr. N. A. Barrett, a retired physician; J. H. Taylor, a real estate man; J. Ellis Brown, a lawyer; H. P. Burruss, a teacher, and J. R. Hornady, a newspaper editor.

This record of economy in the administration of public affairs furnishes a striking contrast to the conditions prevailing prior to the change from the aldermanic to the commission system of government. When this change was made in 1911 there was an annual deficit of over $350,000. Or, to put in more graphic form, the municipality was spending a round thousand dollars a day more than its revenue amounted to. Today few cities in America are upon a firmer financial basis, and its credit is of the best. And good credit, it might be said in passing, is one of the numerous products of efficiency in making the public dollar quit its riotous conduct and settle down to business.

By this reference to the change in the form of government it is not intended to convey the impression that the results obtained are altogether due to the form employed in managing municipal affairs. The form constituted a highly important factor, but the methods used in applying the form were quite as important. A persistent and consistent effort has been made to keep the people informed concerning their public affairs and to enlist their co-operation in mastering the problems that weighed so heavily upon the government during these times of stress.

For a number of years it was my privilege to study the subject of municipal government. I visited a large number of cities having various forms of management, and observed the operation of these several forms at close range. While the impression created was that the commission system is the most effective the primary conclusion was that government, to be conspicuously successful, must be co-operative in character. That is to say, the people, after electing their officials must help them in the management of public affairs.

Speaking broadly, the prevailing attitude of the voters is to take an intense interest in the political side of affairs, and to a large extent ignore the practical aspects of municipal management. They run a regular Fourth of July temperature during the campaign for election of public officials and

TYPICAL SOUTH SIDE HOMES

then fall to zero when it comes to helping those officials make good on their campaign promises. In brief, the average citizen believes that he has discharged his duty towards his town when he leaves the election booth, and his inclination is to let the man on the job look after things for the next two, three or four years, as the case may be.

With this familiar truth in mind, it occurred to me that it would be a most interesting development if a condition were brought about under which public interest would be kept alive between campaigns, and a spirit of genuine co-operation between the people and their officials were created. In due course such an experiment was inaugurated in Birmingham, and the figures quoted above furnish concrete evidence of the results that may be obtained under such conditions.

The five men who constitute the governing body of the City of Birmingham have been unfailing in their efforts to enlist the co-operation of the hundred and forty thousand men and women who constitute the adult population. They have gone out of their way to get the public viewpoint on every important question, and while they have not always followed what appeared to be the popular trend, they have been able to give the people a generally satisfactory reason for going in the other direction. Thus they have fostered the idea of government as an instrumentality of the people; as a thing belonging to them and in which they have a right to be heard other than on election day.

This system has served to keep public interest alive at all seasons. The people know what is going on at the city hall every day in the week, and as a consequence there is little opportunity for the political conspirator to spread sinister rumors and thereby destroy confidence and impair efficiency. People may not always approve what is being done, but they know what is being done and the existence of this knowledge makes a fundamental difference.

Weekly meetings are held by the commissioners, and these meetings are made a clearing house of public opinion. If any important step is contemplated, ample notice is given that the matter is to be considered and all who are interested are invited to be present and give their views.

Following the reading of the proposed ordinance or resolution the subject is thrown open for discussion, and any citizen, male or female, white or black, has the privilege of the floor and the issue is thrashed out from every angle. The commissioners, after listening to the discussion, express their own views, telling why they are for or against the proposed step, and the thing is done. To say that everybody is satisfied would be ridiculous. No attempt is made to satisfy everybody, since this is recognized as impossible, but everybody has a full and fair hearing and the defeated go away feeling that they have had their day in court at any rate.

This method of procedure is a time consumer, but the time so spent has proved to be a splendid investment. The newspapers habitually give considerable space to the discussions, and the public as a whole gets an excellent idea of what is involved in all these questions of public policy. The result is an intimate knowledge of local affairs that tends to keep the people in constant touch with their officials and to keep alive that sense of proprietorship which is essential to successful administration.

It was this highly developed understanding of municipal affairs that made it possible for Birmingham to come through each year of the war with its finances in better condition than at the beginning; this in spite of the tremendous increase in the price of materials and labor. The showing is made more remarkable by the fact that the tax rate in Birmingham until 1921 was the lowest of any city of similar size in America. The average tax rate for municipal purposes in cities of this class is about a dollar and a half on the hundred. In Birmingham the rate was one dollar prior to 1921, and only half of this sum was available for general municipal purposes, thirty cents going to the schools and twenty cents into a sinking fund to care for bonded indebtedness.

Manifestly a city circumscribed in this fashion and confronted by enormously increased costs could not do all that the people wanted done. All it could do without plunging into debt was to perform the essential functions and leave undone the things that were not essential. It was by strict adherence to this policy that the remarkable financial record was achieved. And at this point the value of the co-operative spirit becomes most pronounced. Once shown the impossibility of performing some non-essential thing the public might demand the people conceded the soundness of the position of their officials, and there was comparatively little complaint.

In this connection it may be observed that one of the common causes for deficits in the management of municipal affairs is found in the fact that debts are incurred in order to satisfy the clamor of some element of the citizenship when, if the facts were stated plainly and the citizens were shown what it means to grant such requests, they would in most instances be satisfied to let the matter drop.

I have never known a public official who did not want to please the public, for it is by so doing that he retains his popularity at the polls and is able to continue in office. He is tempted constantly to spend more money than it is wise to expend, and what many officials do not appreciate is the fact that the people who own the government and who ultimately must suffer the consequence of riotous expenditures are reasonable beings and that they are just as ready to applaud sane and judicious management in public affairs as they are in the affairs of the individual. When they criticize and resort to mass meetings because of the failure of the governing body to perform some service that is beyond the financial resources of these officials to perform it is because they are ignorant of the true facts. If they knew the limitations they would no more clamor for these limitations to be exceeded than they would insist upon a business institution with which they might be connected plunging into debts that would inevitably produce bankruptcy.

Having an apt appreciation of these fundamantal truths, the commissioners of Birmingham have kept the spot-light upon public affairs and have been enabled to enlist the sympathetic assistance of the public in meeting the extraordinary difficulties of the past few years. This co-operative spirit not only enabled the city to weather the storms that have arisen, but it has made possible the inauguration of measures of relief for the municipal treasury without which it would have become increasingly difficult to function adequately. The people, knowing all about their government and being in intimate touch with its needs, voted overwhelmingly in favor of such measures of relief as were proposed by their officials. They opened the way for an increase of fifty cents in the tax rate which becomes available for the first time in 1921, and they voted four millions of dollars in bonds for the purpose of providing additional school facilities, additional fire protection, an auditorium and a new city hall.

Such measures of financial relief and such provision for public buildings would never have been provided under the trying conditions then prevailing but for the fact that the majority of people knew all about their government and were satisfied that wisdom and economy would be exercised in handling these largely increased sums. Thus it has been demonstrated beyond peradventure, for the comfort of those who believe in the intelligence of the average American voter in meeting his civic problems that knowledge begets confidence and that confidence makes possible the achievement of large undertakings for the public good.

CHAPTER XVII

ROUTING THE RELUCTANT GERM

WHEN the cholera epidemic of 1873 visited Birmingham there were no sewers, and the first water works system had barely reached completion. Practically the whole population was served from wells which furnished clear and sparkling water but which were heavily polluted, surface closets being the source of contamination. The origin of Asiatic cholera was not known at that time, and the theory arose that it was due to the evil sanitary surroundings. Therefore a vigorous campaign for improved conditions was launched, and coincident therewith was a general abandonment of well water for drinking purposes.

The well which served more people than any other in the community was one that had been provided by the municipality at the intersection of Second Avenue and Nineteenth Street. This well was the Mecca for the thirsty for blocks around, while farmers from far and near slaked their thirst from the old oaken bucket which hung from the spindle. When the epidemic appeared the health authorities became suspicious of this well and caused it to be cleaned out, with results that interested — and nauseated — the community. Tin cans, broken crockery, decaying pieces of rope and many other articles came to the surface, along with a cat and a number of rats.

That water so beautiful could contain so much that was ugly was a surprise to the community, and enterprising individuals who had begun to haul water from neighboring springs and to dispense it at five cents per bucket did a thriving business. This water was hauled in barrels that had done duty as whiskey containers, and one of the earliest recollections of my life is hearing my mother, an uncompromising opponent of the liquor traffic, complain about the odor of whiskey which clung to the water delivered from these springs. Theoretically, this water was pure, but in the light of subsequent discoveries this theory is shown to have been unfounded. It, too, was polluted.

What the people of that period seem not to have

realized was that the limestone with which the valley is so thickly strewn offers little protection against seepage from points of pollution. So they drank the spring water, and when the fright caused by the cholera had subsided returned again to the wells. At that time the construction of cess-pools was permitted, a bad situation being intensified by this practice.

However, the necessity of sewers had become recognized and a substantial beginning was made in this direction. The water works system also was hurried to completion and was ready for service about the time the epidemic subsided. But for a long while only a limited number availed themselves of the opportunity to obtain water from this source.

With the passing of the alarm created at this time, there developed an indifference to sanitary matters that was due in part to the then limited knowledge of bacteria and its influence upon the physical being, but more largely to the fact that the community was experiencing a period of extraordinary stress. The whole nation was in the throes of a benumbing panic and the local situation scarcely could have been worse. Life in Birmingham had become a fight for bare existence, and there was some excuse for the failures of that period. But what can be said in extenuation when the conditions existing up to a few years ago are considered? What excuse can be offered for the fact that for years Birmingham held the unenviable reputation of being one of the most noted centers of typhoid in America? Cases numbered from three to five hundred a year, and practically no attention was paid to it by the general public. Physicians voiced their complaints and sounded their notes of warning, but these warnings received scant notice.

This condition ran on until 1917, when an epidemic of unusual violence broke upon the city, prostrating hundreds within a few weeks. This epidemic was traced to an outside source and local causes were contributory only, but it had the effect of causing a great awakening to the evils of an ancient situation and a sustained effort to eradicate the disease.

It is a well-known fact that something like eight thousand old-fashioned surface closets existed in Birmingham chiefly in unsewered sections, and Dr. R. M. Cunningham, ex-Governor of the State, who was city health officer at the time of the epidemic, had made repeated efforts to eradicate these sources of danger but without success. He uttered repeated warnings concerning what would happen, and when his predictions were verified he threw up the job. Dr. Cecil Gaston, a young physician who subsequently rendered conspicuous service in the hospitals of France during the World War, was called to the position temporarily, and the assistance of the United States Health Service was enlisted. Dr. Lumsden, of the Surgeon General's staff, came here in person, accompanied by a corps of specialists, and in a short time the epidemic was mastered.

In the meantime a plan for the elimination of all old-type surface closets had been worked out by the Commissioner of Health, and the legislation necessary to its execution was obtained. This plan gave the city the right to put in sanitary improvements wherever needed and to assess the cost against the property, the bill being a first lien thereon. Under this system, the proper sanitation of the city progressed with great rapidity, the result being a tremendous decrease in typhoid. While Birmingham is not entirely free from the disease, it may be said that the vanishing point is approaching. That it will disappear is certain, but before the reform can be absolute the sewerage system of the city must be enlarged. Plans for initial enlargements are approaching completion, and the work will be under way in the next few months. The completion of the task will involve expenditures running into the millions, but with the start now being made there is every reason to believe that the improvements will be carried through in the next few years.

The matter of safeguarding the milk supply also has been given exhaustive consideration, and Birmingham has in force regulatory measures embracing the most advanced thought upon this important phase of health conservation.

This long deferred awakening to the importance of health as a community asset and the consequent activities in the suppression of typhoid fever has had an effect that reaches far beyond the original cause. Birmingham has ceased to talk in whispers about the social disease or to attempt a diagnosis in the dark. This disease has been brought out into the clear light of day and its suppression has become the avowed object of a strong organization of patriotic men and women. An intensive educational campaign is being conducted, and the health authorities are receiving the most cordial co-operation in their efforts to minimize the evil.

Here quack nostrums for the treatment of social disease are under strict prohibition. Druggists are not allowed to handle remedies or to attempt cures. As a consequence, the victim must consult a physician, and the law is such that once a treatment is undertaken a cure must be affected before the patient is discharged. The physician must report every case, the patient being designated by a number. If a cure results, then the matter ends; but if the patient fails to continue the treatment until well his name is reported to the Health Department and an officer sees that the treatment is carried to completion.

For notorious women a detention hospital is provided, and here the patients are forced to take the cure. It is interesting to note in this connection that the detention hospital is in a building the use of which is donated by a woman who, before the abolishment of the red-light district years ago, operated it as a house of ill repute. Thus a fountain of disease has become a spring of healing.

Endowed with a climate that is delightful because of the absence of extremes and surrounded by natural conditions which make for healthfulness, Birmingham maintained a low death rate in spite of its high typhoid record, and with the reduction of this disease and the general improvement brought about by the health crusade of the past few years, this record has become even more favorable. In a few years the city should come into prominence as a health resort. Its mountains attain a height of as much as twelve hundred feet above sea level, and with an invigorating atmsophere that swells the lungs and with a view of magnificent distances

CENTRAL HOSPITAL, TENNESSEE COMPANY

that swells the soul it should make a powerful appeal to those whose quest is length of days.

Expenditures by the city and county for health conservation have increased during the past five years from about $20,000 a year to nearly $200,000, one of the results being the creation of a thoroughly equipped laboratory which serves both the city and the county.

Hospitals and infirmaries in and about Birmingham are numerous, well equipped and attractive from an architectural viewpoint, but their number is not sufficient to meet the needs, because of the great influx of patients from other parts of the State. The central location of the city, its excellent railroad facilities and the superior character of its hospitals and infirmaries serve to make Birmingham to Alabamians what the Pool of Siloam was to some of the ancients, and the ill and injured come here in large numbers. The Birmingham Infirmary, the South Highlands Infirmary, the Norwood Infirmary, the Davis Infirmary, the McAdory Infirmary and the Talley Infirmary are chief among the institutions of this character, while the Hillman, the St. Vincent's and the Tennessee are the major hospitals. The latter, a magnificent three million dollar enterprise, is not open to the general public, but cares for many employees of industrial agencies through the district.

There is a children's hospital of limited facilities, and a tuberculosis hospital of inadequate proportions located on Red Mountain. Definite plans for the erection of a new and modern building to house the last-named institution have been formulated, but progress toward fruition is slow and the community justly may be charged with laxity in this matter. A hospital for the treatment of contagious diseases is lacking, and this constitutes another shortcoming that is notable.

The excuse for such failures as exist in Birmingham is youth. The problems of sanitation and drainage and of providing for the elementary necessities of a rapidly growing community have been enormous, and the public revenues have never kept pace with the demands. The surprising thing is not that some important tasks have been left undone, but that so much has been accomplished.

The drainage problem has called for vast expenditures, and millions yet must be spent before the storm water is adequately handled. The valley in which the city is built has a fall so gradual as to be almost imperceptible, and a canal extending many miles beyond the city limits must be provided before the rainwater, rushing down from the mountains, can be carried off promptly and effectively. A great sanitary sewer extending through the valley has been built by the county, but Birmingham has much the same system in the business section that it had thirty years ago when its population was not one-tenth what it is today. This is the system which is to be rebuilt now, but little has been done toward solving the storm sewer problem beyond making surveys. The city has storm sewers, as a matter-of-course, the difficulty being that there is no adequate outlet. However, the fact that matters used to be much worse is illustrated by a story told by Major W. B. Leedy, a pioneer citizen, who presided over the destinies of one of the numerous stock exchanges that flourished here in the boom days.

The practice of the boomers was to buy up acreage somewhere in the vicinity of Birmingham, organize a land company with fabulous amounts of stock, and throw this stock upon the market. Excitement during that boom which came along in the eighties reached a state of frenzy the equal of which rarely has been witnessed, and the mobs about the stock exchange would buy anything that was offered — so long as values leaped upward. When the bottom dropped out and many began to investigate their holdings some melancholy disappointments awaited them. "I went with one man to see what he had bought through a rival exchange," said Major Leedy, "and when he viewed the water under which the land reposed he sighed and remarked, 'I guess we fellows who bought this place will have to raise frogs and utilize the hops for the manufacture of beer.' "

That low-lying section, then far outside the city limits, since has become a part of Birmingham, and today is a busy and populous industrial community, troubled by water occasionally, but in no such condition as when its soggy and abandoned acres proved the undoing of certain money-mad gamblers. So progress has been made in meeting the drainage situation, but mastery of it remains for the future.

In the matter of health conservation the women of Birmingham have been the chief crusaders. They prepared and caused to be passed the first food inspection ordinance, their services in this connection being recognized by the appointment of a woman as chief food inspector. They fought for adequate laws to safeguard the milk supply, and now are engaged in an ambitious effort to minimize the social disease.

However, the activities of Birmingham women have been in no wise limited to civic reforms. It is doubtful if in any community there can be found a larger percentage of women active in commercial and industrial life.

The fourth largest association of business women in America is found in this city, which furnishes conclusive evidence that women have an important part in the development of the material side of the community.

Ina Shepherd is the manager of the Birmingham Clearing House Association, enjoying the distinction of being the only woman holding a like position in the United States. Business ability seems to run in the family, too, for she has a sister who occupies an important position in the office of the City Comptroller, and another sister is Assistant City Clerk.

The business women of Alabama maintain a State organization, and the president, Mrs. H. E. Pearce, has a large business of her own in this city, which she directs while discharging the duties of postmaster of a neighboring town.

Well appointed headquarters are maintained by the business women, where the members may find rest and refreshment, and where topics of interest are discussed by speakers of note. A virile and enthusiastic organization, the Business Women's League, is doing much to foster the interest of the women who lend their talents to the upbuilding of commerce and industry in this district.

In the field of civic endeavor, women had won recognition long before the ballot was obtained under the Nineteenth Amendment. For years women have had representation upon the Board of

Education of the city and county, and upon the Library Board of the city. Similar representation is found on the Art Committee, created by the governing body of the city to advise in the development of the city beautiful idea, and upon the Auditorium Committee, which was created to assist in planning Birmingham's splendid new auditorium, now in course of erection.

The head of the Department of Child Hygiene of the city is a woman, and the supervision of theatrical and motion picture performances by the municipality is in charge of a woman.

In works of relief and correction, women have been pre-eminent. They founded and for years have fostered a refuge for the care of homeless children; a home for wayward girls; a home for aged women; a hospital for children, and numerous other institutions whose value to the community is inestimable. They built up a splendid Young Women's Christian Association, and performed many other services to the struggling girls of the community.

As may be inferred, the presence of a really fine moral atmosphere, in contrast to the loose conditions which existed a quarter of a century ago, has been largely the result of ceaseless activity upon the part of women. Though without the ballot, they were the dominant factor in banishing the saloons, first from Birmingham, and then from the State.

The Boys' Industrial School and the Girls' Industrial School, both of which have become State Institutions and are playing a vital part in correcting the wayward tendencies of the young, were started in this city by women; women who were not satisfied to provide such retreats for the boys and girls of their own community, but labored on until the beneficial influence of these institutions embraced the whole commonwealth. The Boys' Industrial School was established years ago through the tireless labors of Mrs. R. D. Johnston, whose fight for the wayward boys of Alabama did much to arouse the people to the evils which existed at a time when there were no child labor laws, and no child conscience among those who controlled the destinies of the State. She created a public conscience on this score, and thus opened the way for the progress which since has been made in safeguarding the children of the poor whose feet had not gone astray, and in doing a great constructive work in behalf of those who, though erring, may be led into paths of usefulness.

The Girls' School, founded years later through the labors of Mrs. Sam Weakley, is performing a similar service for the girls of the State, after leading for years a struggling existence as a local institution.

The woman whose patient endeavor resulted in the founding of the Mercy Home, a refuge for friendless children, which has been in successful operation for over twenty years, is Mrs. C. B. Spencer. The Octavia White Home for aged women, and the Eva B. Comer Home for working girls, furnish further evidence of the zeal of Birmingham women for the welfare of human kind. Through their labors the Golden Rule has been made concrete.

CHAPTER XVIII

FREAKS OF FRETFUL NATURE

THOUSANDS of years ago, before the earth decided upon a radical re-arrangement of its surface in that territory destined to form the Land of the Free and the Home of the Brave, the section now constituting the mineral district of Alabama was a vast plain, thoroughly on the level but altogether uninteresting.

Had the geologist been known in that remote period, and had he been sent to investigate this district, he might well have made some such report as this to the Exalted Ruler of whatever empire he happened to represent:

"It affords me great pleasure, O King, to have the privilege of conveying to your Most Excellent Highness the information that your humble servant has completed his investigations of the plain about which he was directed to obtain all available information, and he craves the honor of submitting herewith the result of his findings:

"If your Excellency will picture in your mind an immense layer cake, such as mother used to make, a fairly accurate idea of what I shall attempt to describe may be obtained. For the top layer, which usually is coated white with some sweet confection, imagine a great waste of sand, practically level. This sand coat covers about half of the territory which will become known as Alabama, following the founding of that great country to be known as the United States of America.

"Beneath the layer of sand, and extending to a great depth, is a layer of conglomerate material which might be described as of the earth earthy. Then, like golden coins in a wedding cake, come layers of great value — layers of coal, of iron ore and of rock, such as limestone and dolomite, which will prove to be excellent fluxing materials when tossed within reach of the men who are to build furnaces in the city which is to be founded here and which will be known as Birmingham.

"These layers of minerals are far beneath the surface of the plain, the iron ore being perhaps a mile below the spot where I have pitched my tent, and the possibility of these materials becoming useful factors in the industrial life of the world would be very remote but for the fact that nature plans some extraordinary convulsions in this vicinity. During this process, the lower layers of our cake will be pushed to the top, where man may reach and do with them what he will.

"All of which is respectfully submitted, with the hope that the shadow of your Highness will never grow less."

With this report before us, it becomes necessary merely to record that the "convulsion of nature" occurred in due season, resulting in great sections of the extraordinary mineral cake being pushed to the surface. This convulsion became known as the Appalachian revolution, and the best friend of the North American continent would not have recognized it after the completion of the pushing process. A chain of mountains was thrown up, extending from Canada to Central Alabama, and in this quarter the once level land became as choppy as a storm-tossed sea.

A quantity of the iron in the cake of the ancient geologist was thrown up to become Red Mountain, while segments of iron and coal flew hither and yon, creating a sort of marble-cake effect, when viewed in connection with the numerous and far-reaching slabs of limestone and dolomite that were tossed about.

One might infer that this disposition of the minerals made their utilization a sort of holiday enterprise, and much that has been written tends to perpetuate an impression of this kind, but candor compels the admission that certain difficulties stood in the way; difficulties that required the utmost ingenuity and perseverence to overcome, even in part.

As an illustration, consider the coal vein. The prospector finds a beautiful slice of that old-time layer cake, and bores into it gleefully. Ton after ton of the shining black stuff is dug out and hauled to the surface, and everything is going lovely. Then, on some melancholy day, the end comes with startling abruptness. The coal gives out and a wall of rock stands in the way.

This means that a "fault" has been reached, and not that the mine has to be abandoned, for the owner knows that a continuation of the layer he has been working is somewhere in the vicinity. He begins, therefore, to bore and to dig until he finds the continuation. Sometimes it is found fifty feet higher up, sometimes a hundred feet lower down. Then the intervening rock must be cut away, and the new deposit of coal linked up with the openings into the old.

A striking illustration of how these once uniform layers of coal were broken up by the Appalachian revolution may be observed at the Edgewater mines of the Tennessee Company, opened in 1911. Here there is a difference of one hundred feet in the two levels, nature having, at this point, broken the layer of coal squarely in two and thrust one section high up, while depositing the other a hundred feet lower down. Then, as if determined to create just as much confusion as possible in the brain of the mining engineer, she varied the process further along by tossing one side of the lower strata high up, and burying the opposite side of the higher strata deep in the earth.

At the mine in question, the problem of hauling coal from the two levels was mastered by digging vertical shafts side by side. Elevators operate in these shafts, suspended by steel cables that pass over immense drums, so arranged that one elevator moves more rapidly than the other, resulting in the separate lifts reaching their separate underground destinations at the same moment, though standing side by side when on the surface.

Next to the Bayview mine, owned by the same company, Edgewater is the most modern mine in Alabama. The coal when brought up from the two levels at the same moment, is dumped directly upon a conveyor which carries it to the crusher, the rock and slate being picked out while the coal is in transit. From the crusher, the coal goes to the washer, where it undergoes a three-fold process of separation, the best being dumped into cars which stand below the washer. This coal is hauled to the by-product plant for conversion into coke. The inferior, or steam coal, is dumped on the ground for use in a pumping plant that stands nearby, and from which flows the great volume of water required in the operation of the furnaces, steel mills and by-product plants, which form a vast chain of industries in that territory.

In addition to playing all kinds of tricks with the coal seams, nature, as if repenting of her prodigality in this district, proceeded to throw a bit too much stone, sulphur and ash into the coal mixture, thereby making extra work for the chemists and metallurgists, and presenting all sorts of complications when the effort was made to do with this coal what was being done with coals of Illinois, Ohio, Pennsylvania and West Virginia.

These facts are recited for the purpose of showing that the tremendous development brought about in the coal fields of Alabama meant real work on the part of real men. This field is not and has never been a place for weaklings. As the pioneers had to struggle and scheme, first to find a process for making coke out of Alabama coal, and then for some means of converting Alabama iron into steel, so the men who are at work today in developing the resources of the district have to battle with difficulties all along the way. The thing that makes possible their triumphs — and their triumphs have been numerous and of far-reaching significance — is the proximity of the materials with which they work.

As the coal plays queer freaks, so with the ore, and here, too, the call is for resourcefulness and ingenuity. Instead of the ore being deposited on the surface in great pits, as is the case in some quarters, it lies in veins which must be followed far into the earth, in some instances necessitating frequent supports for overhanging roof, and long lines of narrow-gauge roads for hauling the ore to the surface. And when delivered to the surface, this ore cannot be expected to produce, ton for ton, as much iron as is produced in fields where the metallic content is greater. It is not a strictly high grade ore, and the fact that it is made to produce a high grade steel furnishes an excellent testimonial to the skill and resourcefulness of the men who smelt it and work the product into superior metal.

The quality of Birmingham steel having been established, and the metal being accepted without question, the development of the industry has become one of demand in the territory which best may be served from Birmingham. This includes a large part of the South, Mexico, Central and South America, and countries lying beyond the Panama Canal.

Steel is a general term, like fruit or vegetables. There are many kinds of fruit and a great variety of vegetables, and this also is true of steel. When one wishes to be specific about the price of fruit or vegetables, he asks "How much are oranges?" or "What is the price of cabbage?" And so one must be specific when it comes to steel. The question "How much is steel selling for?" might be answered in a thousand different ways. A pound of watch springs is worth about $4,000, while a pound of bar steel is worth about two cents. Between these extremes are many intermediate grades, representing varying products.

The production of steel involves the production of an ingot — a rough, box-like slab which passes white-hot into the rollers to emerge in the shape best adapted to the purpose for which it is intended.

A steel ingot varies in composition in accordance with the kind and quality of steel to be made from it, as dough varies according to what is expected to come from the oven. Generally speaking, the cost of the ingot does not as a rule vary between different localities as much as does the

cost of the product into which it is converted. The cost of converting an ingot into a steel bar may vary as much as two or three times in amount, depending upon the volume of business and the degree to which specialization in rolling is made possible.

The simplest form of mill for rolling steel bars is that which is known to the craft as a "Merchant Mill." This mill has a range of sizes greater than is possessed by other types, and one of fair proportions will roll approximately 2,500 tons of steel bars per month. By "range" is meant the size of the product coming from the rolls, the size varying, as a matter of course, according to the character of the orders on hand. The production of varying sizes and shapes by the same mill is made possible through the substitution of rolls. A set of rolls having the shape of the familiar rolling pin with which every kitchen is equipped would produce flat steel, but take the same rollers and cut a half circle in them, and they will produce round bars, the size being determined by the size of the completed circle. The process is not quite so simple as this might appear, since the shapes are not produced by a single set of rolls, but this will serve to give some idea of the way in which the Merchant Mill functions in converting the ingot into the steel shape.

To the novice there are few things more wonderful than to watch the operation of one of these mills, equipped with its many pairs of gigantic "rolling pins." The steel ingot, usually about twenty inches square and six feet long, rushes upon the first set of rollers and is squeezed through, being flattened somewhat in the passage. Immediately upon leaving the rolls, the ingot reverses its course and returns for another squeeze. As it rushes back to the starting point, it is turned on edge and darts again through the rolls. This process continues until the girth has been considerably reduced and the length greatly extended. Then the mass moves on to other rolls, continuing the journey until it is more than a hundred feet in length. The ragged ends are then cut off by giant blades, and the bar is ready for the finishing rolls. Still hot and pliable, it reaches the rolls where the final shape is to be given, and presently is transformed into a steel rail of enormous length. This rail is then sawed into standard sizes for railroad building, the sawing process creating a fireworks display that would be creditable to any Fourth of July celebration. Then the rails are ready for straightening, cooling and drilling. After passing through these processes, the rails are ready for delivery to the railroad builder, and giant electric magnets pick them up and load them upon the flat cars that stand in long lines outside the mill.

The rolls upon a merchant mill are changed to meet the varying demands. And herein is the difference between such a mill and the mill which is termed "specialized." The latter is built in anticipation of enormous orders for a few articles and is not subject to constant changes, as is the merchant mill. Now enters the tremendously important item of production cost. A specialized mill, being subject to few stoppages for changes, and geared to meet certain predetermined conditions, produces a much larger tonnage than is possible with a merchant mill. Thus, if four specialized mills are provided, each to turn out one-fourth of the shapes produced by the more flexible but slower merchant mill, these four plants would be capable of turning out 10,000 tons each per month, or an aggregate of 40,000 tons, as compared to the 2,500 tons produced by the merchant mill.

The initial cost of the specialized mill is about twice that of the merchant mill, but as it rolls about four times the tonnage, the investment cost is only one-half as much per ton produced.

Where the market for steel products is such that specialized mills may be operated, it is obvious that the manufacturer has a distinct advantage over the one whose wide range of products must be made in a single mill. The specialist has cut his conversion cost half in two and has performed the same operation upon his investment cost. At the same time, however, he has created a condition under which he must produce an enormously greater output than the merchant mill operator, which means that he must have a market whose capacity for consumption is proportionately large. Otherwise he loses the advantage of top-notch production.

The wage element is an important factor in the comparative cost of operating merchant mills and specialized mills. A specialty mill running at half its capacity must have men just as skilled as those employed in the full-time merchant mill, and it cannot maintain a lower production cost under such circumstances. Its job is to keep busy.

Birmingham's range of specialized mills is not large as yet, though existing plants are enormous in extent. The encouraging thing is that such mills are found at all in a district so new to the steel industry. Moreover, they are prophetic of new conquests in the markets of the world. They are significant of the time when the nations to the South, and those lying beyond the Panama Canal, will have an adequate appreciation of the value of steel; of its permanency, of its adaptability and of its cheapness, as compared to the more perishable products.

The measure of growth Birmingham has attained as a steel center has come about largely within the last dozen years, expansion upon a huge scale beginning with the entry of the United States Steel Corporation upon its absorption of the Tennessee Coal, Iron & Railroad Company under the administration of President Roosevelt. This organization has spent with a lavish hand in the modernization of old plants and in the erection of new ones, and under its progressive policy the district has grown at a pace which would have been impossible without the presence of an agency so well equipped, mentally and financially, to master the production problems and meet the market conditions existing in this territory.

Speaking of growth, recalls an amusing incident that occurred some years ago at a dinner attended by the representative steel men of America. At that time both Birmingham and Chicago had extended their corporate limits in such a way as to take in considerable territory, and this fact was fresh in the mind of at least one gentleman present. During the evening the conversation turned to Birmingham and Chicago, both destined to greatness as steel centers, and much was said about the way in which the two cities were growing. After listening to this line of conversation for some time, Frank Bachus arose and convulsed the crowd by saying:

"I have watched the growth of Birmingham and Chicago with great interest and have gone far enough into the subject to give some absolutely accurate figures. These figures show that if Birmingham and Chicago continue to grow at the same percentage for the next fifty years as they have during the past fifty years their corporate limits will meet at Evansville, Indiana!"

The Birmingham contingent pretended to find some satisfaction in the delicate suggestion thus conveyed that this city was "growing" a bit faster than the Illinois metropolis, even though the growth was territorial rather than in the numbers of its people.

As a matter of fact, Birmingham's limits were extended in 1910 to include a number of near-by communities, and the city today embraces fifty square miles. At that, the largest industrial plants are not within the corporate limits but just outside, the lines having been drawn so in order to relieve these huge enterprises of the burden of municipal taxation and at the same time lend encouragement to similar enterprises which might be induced to locate in this territory.

CHAPTER XIX

THE TEETH OF A CHILD

DURING the preparation of this work I have climbed to the top of lofty tipples where the coal came roaring along in an endless stream and where the earth seemed to tremble as the crushers crumbled the lumps to dust. I have stood upon the peak of giant washers where hundreds of tons of coal were hurried through various processes by endless chains whose wide scoops splashed and clanked as they swept on and on; I have been deep in the earth where hundreds of men bored their way into the jet black veins, and where laden cars crashed by hurrying to the exits; I have stood amid the heat and din of giant furnace plants and have watched the serpentine performance of great bars of ruddy steel as they twisted and squirmed the length of roaring mills; I have seen skyscrapers and stores of vast proportion and have viewed beautiful thoroughfares and magnificent homes, but amid all the mighty panorama the picture most vividly impressed upon my mind is that of two rows of white shining teeth between two ruddy, laughing lips; the teeth and the lips of a little daughter of the mines.

The picture presented by that laughing child lingers because it is significant of something big, and fine, and compelling; something that is more inspiring than all the mills and furnaces and sky-piercing buildings that man may erect. It is the token of a high purpose upon the part of great industrial agencies to put first the conservation of human life and human happiness; the visible expression of a new-age ideal on the part of employers.

That the same concern which bores deep into the earth to bring forth coal; that erects huge furnaces and operates mills and factories covering miles of ground, and which pushes its trade conquests into the far places of the earth, takes time to consider the teeth of a little child is a development which points again to the fact that the fires in the heart of industrial Birmingham are lighted from the soul.

The co-ordination which exists in this field of

conservation is just as striking and just as efficient as it is in the field of industrial endeavor. As inter-dependent plants have been located in a manner which guarantees the maximum of efficiency, so every step in the great scheme of safeguarding human beings has been worked out with a view of eliminating lost motion and to achieving the highest possible results.

With the greatest of the industrial agencies at work in the Birmingham district, the heart of the conservation system is a three million dollar hospital, standing upon an eminence from which may be viewed the wide panorama of Birmingham. There are some hospitals in America larger than this, but none more complete. In every appointment, from the huge bakery on the ground floor rear to the great, tile-lined operating rooms on the upper floor, this hospital is complete in the most minute detail. The evidence of lavish expenditures is seen on every hand, the general effect being that of a magnificent hotel rather than a place to care for the ill and the injured. The wide, sweeping roof of the structure forms an outdoor garden where the convalescents may sit or stroll in the sunshine and feast their eyes upon a cyclorama that can never grow tiresome. A valley teaming with life is spread before them, while in the distance vague and misty hills invite and rest the eye. Dr. Lloyd Nolan, a distinguished surgeon, is in charge of this hospital.

Connected with this central hospital, and in instant communication therewith, are large numbers of emergency hospitals and first-aid stations, these auxiliary institutions being found at every industrial plant, at every mining camp, and down in the mines themselves.

Injured are given first-aid treatment in these local stations, after which, if the hurts are serious, they are placed in ambulances and hurried to the central hospital, there to receive the best attention that unlimited means can provide.

But caring for the injured is only a minor function in the operation of this far-reaching piece of conservation machinery. To keep the body whole and in a fit condition is the big ideal behind it all.

This company has trained nurses, physicians and sanitary experts in every camp, and in cooperation with the county it operates the public schools. The buildings are light, airy and sanitary, and the children are observed with watchful care. If defects of any kind are observed, the nurse reports it to the physician and then the whole resources of the organization are at the disposal of that child. Even the most remote camp is visited regularly by the company dentists, and every person with defective teeth has his or her day of opportunity. In all of these schools daily "tooth-brush drills" are held, with the result that the era of bad molars is fast disappearing. The daughter of the mining camp of today is not like the one of olden times, who, when reminded that her teeth were decaying, replied by saying, "I hope they'll last until I get married." Today the young folks in the mining camps have a livelier hope than this.

The absence of a child is noted at once in these schools and inquiry is made immediately. If the case proves one in which some disease has developed the fact is reported by the visitor, a trained community worker, and the physician goes at once. If is proves to be a contagious disease, precautions are taken to prevent its spread. If it is something requiring a high order of skill in combatting, the visitor goes to the hospital, there to receive the same attention that would be showered upon a millionaire.

In the baby ward on the colored side of that great central hospital I saw a number of ebony tots, their black skin shining against the snow-white linen, and they were receiving the same skillful attention that was being given the patients at the other end of the big structure. Some were suffering from mal-nutrition when discovered and taken to the hospital, and here their food was being weighed and measured and their poor, misshapen forms were being coaxed into healthfulness.

Much has been said and written about the "Whittling negro," meaning the one who dearly likes to apply a keen-edged knife to a piece of soft pine, but I never realized how great this passion for cutting could become until I saw the performance of a negro boy in this hospital. He had been caught in an automobile wreck and was himself about as complete a wreck as ever appeared in a hospital. His left arm was broken in two places, both legs were broken at sundry points, and his head was a mass of bruises. When I saw him he was trussed up in a most amazing fashion. His legs were raised high above his head, splinted and weighted, and his left arm was arranged in similar fashion, the hand alone being free, and its measure of freedom being limited to a slight movement of the fingers. Yet this human wreck held a piece of soft pine in that trussed-up hand, by those sadly circumscribed fingers, and, reaching high up with the one uninjured limb, he was deftly whittling at that piece of wood!

I laughed outright at the absurdity of the thing, and the darky chuckled in return but did not miss a stroke with his busy little knife.

The work of reaching and helping the children in these industrial communities is one which brings the worker in frequent contact with the home, and for this reason it is entrusted to women. Skillful, diplomatic and well-trained, they are performing a miracle of usefulness in many quarters. The result of such activities will be to put the children of the mining camps far ahead of the children of other small communities, unless there is a more general awakening in these sections to the importance of conserving human materials.

The same reasons that impel great industrial agencies to spend large sums in promoting the mental and bodily welfare of the children in the communities where their money is invested should impel the thoughtful citizens of every center of population, however small, to encourage similar activities. Decent schools, where the mind may be developed under properly equipped instructors; playgrounds, where the bodily development may be made to keep pace with the growth of the mind, and adequate means for the correction and prevention of physical defects, should be a part of the equipment of every community. Until this condition is brought about, the average small town will continue to be put to shame by the modern mining camp just as the old-time camp is put to shame by the same remarkably efficient institution.

When one views the well-equipped playgrounds,

the large and attractive community clubs, the public bath houses and schools, and observes the precautions that are taken to safeguard the lives and the health of the people in these camps, it is to wonder when a like situation will materialize in those far more numerous communities where the reliance is upon public money rather than upon private capital. The thought is irresistible that if far-off investors find it profitable to spend money in this wise through their officials, it should be equally profitable for those whose lives are spent in small towns to make similar investments through their public officials.

Slowly, perhaps, but surely, some such sentiment as this is going to develop through the urge and precept of example. Signs of it are seen in the growing demand throughout Alabama for improved educational facilities. It has been less than half a dozen years since the Constitution of the State was amended permitting the various counties and the school districts within these counties to levy as much as three mills additional for school purposes. This amendment was carried only after the most heart-breaking labor, many counties in the State voting against it. Yet, within so short a time as since has intervened, every county in the State has seen the wisdom of increasing school funds, while scores of school districts voted additional increases after the county had acted. This growing appreciation of educational advantages, accompanied as it is by enlarging facilities, is the most hopeful sign of the times.

An analysis of the actuating motives behind that which, to the casual observer, might be construed as philanthropic activities on the part of great industrial institutions, forms an interesting study. Broadly speaking, these activities spring from a desire to create and to hold an intelligent and contented working force, accompanied by a sense of genuine responsibility for the welfare of employees.

In the application of this theory of how to create and hold an experienced and efficient force, some very remarkable results have been obtained along cultural as well as practical lines. Music and the drama have been made to flourish along with sound teeth and a sound body. The pageant is very popular, and it is not unusual for whole communities to become so interested in the presentation of a great, spectacular performance that all other topics are forgotten. Mothers become lost in the task of creating wonderful costumes for children who are to appear as fairies or flowers, or for adults who are to impersonate heroic figures in some dramatic master-piece. For such presentations the company furnishes the skilled director and the community furnishes the talent and the enthusiasm essential to success.

Through affairs of this kind there has been built up in more than one community a wholesome pride in the "home town" that has had an almost electrical effect upon the attitude of the people. I shall never forget the interest and enthusiasm which attended the presentation of a wonderfully elaborate pageant at one of the old ore mines in the Birmingham district.

The excuse for this spectacular production was the changing of the name of the camp; the change being from something commonplace and meaningless to something classic and suggestive — something that would appeal to the imagination of the resident and give him a prideful talking point when visitors came to town.

The legend about the new name was developed by the dramatic director in such a way that practically the whole population was brought into the production, and never was greater interest manifested in an event of the kind. As illustrating the measure of this interest, it may be chronicled that an aged blacksmith who had been overlooked in the organization of the pageant came forward and demanded the privilege of having some part in it. Just what to do with him was a problem for a time, but he offered the solution by declaring that he was going to be "the iron man" of the show, and he was. The measure of his interest may be gauged by the fact that in creating his costume and equipment he even went to the length of making a special sledge hammer with his own hands. Large of body and seared by years of contact with the metal he represented, this old blacksmith made a heroic figure when the spectacle was produced.

When this pageant finally was presented one starry night there was a great multitude on hand to witness it, the spectators including a large number of people from Birmingham who had gone out upon a special train. A vast and colorful spectacle, presented with skill born of long practice and with an enthusiasm which bore eloquent testimony to the interest of the participants, the event was a huge success.

While pageants so elaborate and so all-embracing as this are somewhat rare, smaller productions are commonplace and always they are events of great interest in the communities where they are presented. Even the colored camps are not immune from the contagion of the pageant, and another picture I have in mind is a group of perhaps fifty little colored girls all attired as "fairies" and all wearing costumes of filmy white, adorned with gossamer wings. While black-faced fairies call for some strain upon the imagination, and there is something in such a spectacle that tends to provoke a smile, there also is something that grips the heartstrings, for these dusky children of the hills are just as much in earnest and find just as much delight in their work as is found by the dainty little beauties who perform in like fashion in the camps of the Caucasians.

Exquisite settings for the presentation of pageants are found in almost every community throughout the mining district, the hills being richly wooded as a rule, and present many charming glens and hill-side stages. To see a crowd of beautiful children adorned with filmy costumes performing their graceful evolutions upon one of these stages which nature has so artistically decorated is to get a new conception of the ideals toward which men and women and industrial institutions are striving in the mineral regions of Alabama.

To conclude that these ideals dominate in all the mining camps would be to err most grievously, for such is not the case. There are camps here and there, and industrial communities here and there, where the settings and surroundings are commonplace enough, and where life contains few colorful aspects. But the point is that they represent an order that is passing. The new camp, with its attention to the mental, physical and social, as well as the spiritual life, is representa- tive of the trend today. The old order is passing; the new order moves with quickened tread.

CHAPTER XX

ALADDIN'S LAMP SURPASSED

IN no branch of industry is the skill and ingenuity of man demonstrated more impressively than in that field in which he hies forth to gather the color and the nectar and the elusive fragrance of flowers and fruits that blossomed and ripened and died long centuries ago.

Fancy, if you will, a tropical forest, luxuriant with growth. Giant trees rear their heads and stretch long arms that interlock and form deep and shady lanes. Vines, like monster serpents, trail their tortuous way from trunk to limb and tree to tree, their tendrils twining in and out and their clustered fruits dotting the forest with purple and yellow and red. In open spaces, where the sunlight finds its way, fruit trees flourish, bearing first the blossom, with its delicate shades and its sweet perfumes; and then the ripened fruit, with its varying degrees of loveliness and its wide diversity of flavor.

Flowers, too, bloom here, splashing the forest with color as the sunset splashes the evening sky, and filling the air with fragrance; the fragrance of the violet, subtle and sweet; of the wild rose, so elusive as scarcely to be detected, and of the yellow jessamine, strong and persuasive.

Herbs with many remarkable medicinal qualities grow in this forest, too, and there are plants which contain gases, oils and acids, alkalis and similar properties, in endless variety.

With such a scene as this upon the mental screen, then fancy the passing of many centuries, with their amazing changes in the contour and conditions upon the earth's surface. The forest, with its riot of life and color and fragrance, has been buried beneath billions of tons of ice and snow. It has been subjected to mighty pressure, to the grinding action of great, slow moving weights, to floods, and to the changing processes of the ages.

Time passes, millions of years perhaps, and the substance of what once constituted that forest is buried deep in the earth, a black, hard mass, varying in thickness from a few feet to ten and twelve feet in rare instances. This mass is called bituminous coal.

It is into the remains of this prehistoric forest that the scientist goes upon his remarkable expeditions and returns with the evidence of such amazing conquests. Every element that entered into the making of that long-lost forest is recovered. The color of the grape, the sweet of the plum, the fragrance of the violet, the bitter of the medicinal herb, the gas of the decaying growth, the oil of the nut; these, and thousands of other elements, are recovered, and, behold, the forest appears; appears in the color of the lawn, worn by the little miss; in the shade of the tie about her father's neck; in the tints upon the veil the mother wears upon her face; in the perfume on the dresser and the flavoring extract upon the shelf; in the drugs stored up in the medicine case and in the polish that awaits application to boots and shoes; in the gas that cooks the dinner and in the streets over which the food is hauled; in the roof upon the housetop and the colors of paint upon the walls.

Every element in that once luxuriant forest is recovered; the flower that bloomed unseen in ages gone is made to bloom again, and so with all the rest of it. But for this amazing miracle, which forms one of the greatest tributes that can be paid to the ingenuity of man, the world would be quite a different sort of place, lacking much in color, in beauty, in convenience, and in things that minister to the comfort and the health of its inhabitants.

Some of the common uses to which the by-products of coal are put include the manufacture of steel, paints, oils, fertilizers, baking sodas, chemical supplies, medicines, explosives, dyes, fruit preservatives, soaps, oil stains, washing powders, photographic supplies, insulation for electrical appliances, glass making, illuminating and cooking gas, waterproofing and wood preservatives. The refinements run into the thousands, entering practically every industry under the sun.

While the old-fashioned bee-hive oven, which made coke and nothing else, was used exclusively in Birmingham for a number of years, and all the precious by-products were allowed to go to waste, serious attention began to be given this subject some twelve or fifteen years ago, and in cousequence several large by-product plants have been erected, their aggregate output covering a wide range. Among the earliest enterprises of this character was the Semet-Solvay plant, forming one of the immense group of inter-dependent industries in the Ensley field. The latest enterprise is the Sloss by-product plant, famed as the starting point of national and international balloon races, and the plant from which Birmingham obtains its gas for lighting and heating purposes.

The tree, symbolic of that ancient forest, furnishes an excellent illustration of the stages through which the various elements in coal are developed, though processes vary with varying institutions.

With this fanciful tree growing out of a bed of coal, we will name the main trunk "gas," and the first big limb protruding from it "ammonia liquor." From this limb there are a multitude of off-shoots, the derivatives of which may be enumerated in this wise: ammonium phosphate, ammonium chloride (used in batteries and in galvanizing), ammonium oxalate, ammonium tartrate, soda ash, ammonium carbonate, ammonium bicarbonate (used in baking and in washing compounds), aqua ammonia, household ammonia, anhydrous ammonia (used in refrigeration), cyanide, ammonia sulphate (used in making fertilizers), ammonium bromide, ammonium nitrate (used in making explosives), ammonium sulphocyanide, ammonium fluride, ammonium alum, and ammonium iodide.

On the opposite side of this tree fancy a larger limb, with a number of rather large off-shoots. This limb we will name "tar," and, taking up the first off-shoot, called "pitch," we find insulation, paints, waterproofing, roofing, paving, core compounds, füel, and electrodes. Branching off, opposite this secondary limb, is one which may be called "refined tar," producing paints, wood preservatives, roofing, waterproofing, pipe coating and paving materials. Another limb, called "light oil," and we find benzol and its derivatives, phenol and its derivatives, toluol and its derivatives, emulsions, cresol, disinfectants, insecticides, germicides, denaturing agents, naphtha, para cumadone, varnish, etc. Another robust off-shoot from this "tar" limb may be called "middle oil," some of the derivatives of which are phenol, cresol, paint thinners, wood preservatives, shingle stains, printing ink, lampblacks, shoe polishes, naphthalene, sundry drugs and acids, dyes and explosives. At the end of this same robust limb, where the heavy oils flow, the chemist finds more lampblack, more wood preservatives, anthracene oil, cholorinated oils, and an elaborate collection of dyes.

Another large limb with multiple off-shoots is called "crude benzol," and here may be found toluol, nitro toluols to ludine, benzyl chloride, more explosives and more dyes, saccharine (its presence here showing that it is without food value), benzaldehyde, perfumes, food preservatives, more drugs, anesthetics, benzoyl chloride, xylol, nitro xylols, xylidines, solvent naphtha, rubber cement, resrocin, sulpho acids, phenol, picric acid, picrates, more explosives, antiseptics, anisol, more drugs, more disinfectants, sulpho acid, artificial leather, and more drugs, dyes and solvents.

Toward the top of the main trunk of the imaginary tree will be found residual gas with offshoots of sulphur, sulphurous acid, carbon disulphide, viscos, sundry drugs, cyanogen, cyanide, ammonia, nitric acid, ferrocyanide, pigments, prussian blue, photographic chemicals, chemicals for gold recovery, gas for domestic uses, for glass furnaces, for open-hearth furnaces, steam boilers, etc., and, at the very top, carbon black.

These various elements of common use constitute but a few of the many valuable properties recovered from bituminous coal. Practically all of the by-products mentioned here are subject to refinement that lead to the production of many other things found in every-day use, from which it is clear that without the remains of those ancient forests, and without the ability of man to recover the elements of which they were composed, the world would be a much less attractive, less healthful and less colorful place in which to live; a world lacking much in the conveniences that go to make life pleasant. Indeed, the exclamation of the sweet young girl who cried, "Oh, isn't nature cute!" upon first beholding the marvels of the Grand Canyon, scarcely expresses the feeling of one who considers the marvelous character of the black and shining substance which burns upon the grate when winter's winds are blowing. It is a magic lamp, far more wonderful than the fabled lamp of old.

As nature has assembled the raw materials at the doors of Birmingham's industrial enterprises, so man has performed feats of co-ordination that are remarkable in their completeness. This is found in the location of by-product plants in relation to enterprises consuming the various elements extracted from coal. In the Ensley group of industries, underground pipes convey materials from the by-product plants to industrial enterprises which consume or convert these elements. Thus tar, which forms the base of all the materials produced at the plant of the Barrett Manufacturing Company, is piped direct from the point of origin, there to be converted into road materials, roofing materials, paints and other products of like character.

Adjoining this plant are three immense lakes of material which is called "pitch," and which represents the residue of tar after the sundry elements have been extracted. These lakes, the largest of their kind in the world, cover many acres and are as much as thirty feet deep in some places. Practically worthless as they stand, they represent the ever-present problem involved in the

BY-PRODUCT PLANT. NAVAL AIR CRAFT JUST LEAVING

utilization of waste products. This pitch is capable of being converted into the finest of coke, but no process has been devised for converting it into this highly useful material upon a basis that would be profitable, though many thousands of dollars have been expended in the building of experimental ovens and in carrying on various researches. So the material piles up, flowing from the furnaces in liquid form and becoming hard and brittle when exposed to the air. A small quantity of it is being used in France in the manufacture of fuel, but beyond this there is no demand for it.

It has been in the mastery of problems such as that presented by the presence of this huge volume of refuse, that industry has gone forward to new conquests, and, as in the case of slag, there is no doubt but the inquiring mind and the restless hand of the chemical engineer will yet touch upon some means of utilizing this material. And, in so doing, will open up new avenues of industrial activities.

Within a short distance of these lakes of pitch is found evidence upon which prophecy with reference to waste products is justified, for here slag is being converted into brick and tile.

Slag is the refuse which comes from furnaces after the metallic iron has been removed from the ore mixture. As great mountains of sawdust once accumulated around every sawmill, so giant heaps of slag grew about furnaces. These heaps grew and grew with the passing of the years and came to encumber hundreds of acres that might have been utilized for other purposes. Coming from the furnaces in a molten state, the slag is run into great vessels, mounted upon trucks, and these vessels are pulled or pushed to the top of the mountains by engines. There they are tilted, and the slag rolls down the sides like lava from the mouth of a white-hot volcano. Thus the mountains have grown, until today there are many millions of tons of the material scattered over the Birmingham district.

Until recent years, this material was considered worthless. Then cities and towns began to use small quantities of it in road building, as has been pointed out elsewhere. Coincidentally, railroad contractors found that it was peculiarly adapted to the building of roadbeds, and bridge builders and house builders discovered that it was ideal for foundation work. The development of these uses created a market for much of the material, but it merely marked the beginning, for experiments were being made in many directions, and presently new industries, based upon the utilization of slag for building materials, sprang up.

The brick and tile plant to which reference is made here is located within the shadow of the huge battery of furnaces at Ensley. There, instead of the slag being piled up in mountains, as was the case for so many years, it is thrown out convenient to the brick and tile works where it is consumed by one process or another.

A process has been discovered for giving a smooth finish to the exposed surface of the slag brick and the slag tile, and of imparting to it any color, or combination of colors, that may be suggested. Thus many beautiful effects are obtained, and thus a great and useful industry has been founded upon a material that was little more than a nuisance a few years ago. Other uses are found for slag in other industrial plants, and, as this is written, plans are under way for converting it into snow-white bathtubs, into huge vases, glorified with every color of the rainbow, and into many other useful and ornamental products. Thus the despised slag pile has become a mountain of potential wealth; the basis of many and varied enterprises and the means of providing many hands with tasks not dreamed of in other days.

Another interesting plant from which comes a slag by-product of great value is found in the midst of this group of busy industries clustered about the battery of furnaces at Ensley. This is a fertilizer plant, producing basic phosphate, which is the best soil food known because it carries no acid and corrects the acid in the soil with which it comes in contact. In this plant the machinery is so co-ordinated that two men can turn out 7,100 bags in ten hours. The slag from which this fertilizer is made is not the ordinary blast-furnace slag, but is a special product of the open-hearth furnace, growing out of the duplex process of manufacturing steel, and is exceptionally rich in phosphorous.

While most of the gigantic industries of Birmingham are grouped in this territory, where the iron may take a running start, leap through the steel mill, and then whirl into the establishment where it goes into the finished product, there are other districts in which diversified industries of almost every conceivable character are found.

Forming a great crescent, which circles East Birmingham and extends through North Birmingham, may be found an immense number of establishments consuming quantities of iron and steel and employing many thousands of skilled mechanics. Sugar mills, so huge that it requires an entire train to haul a single plant, locomotives, stationary engines, steamship engines, ship fittings, boilers, cotton gins, stoves, radiators, clay pipe, pipe fittings, and many other products are manufactured in this territory. Then there are more furnaces, another steel plant, an automobile factory, cotton seed mills, bolt and nut works, lumber yards, planing mills, grate factories, machine shops and foundries extending mile upon mile.

Turning west from North Birmingham and bending again in the direction of Ensley, comes a huge clay pipe and tile plant, a tremendous iron pipe plant which, with the stores and schools and homes about it, constitutes a town in itself, and a model town it is. Here, in Acipco, even the humblest negro worker has a home equipped with bath and all modern appliances for comfort and health. Further on, still moving in the direction of Ensley, one comes to the great and modern furnace plant of the Republic Iron & Steel Company — occupying the center of another community where flowers bloom along the streets and where ample evidence is found of a desire to surround the worker with the things that go to make home life attractive.

Next in order comes Pratt City (though we are still within the confines of Birmingham), and here are found other openings into the great Pratt coal seam. The first opening into this seam was made at this point in 1878 when the problem of obtaining a sufficient amount of coal to provide coke for the iron furnaces was most urgent. Though the means of making Birmingham iron by the coke process had been discovered only a couple of years before, many new furnaces had been projected, and the shortage of coal had become acute. H. F. DeBardeleben and J. W. Sloss, both of whom had been active in developing the coke iron industry, became associated with T. H. Aldrich, another pioneer developer, and the trio made the initial opening into the seam, which since that date has penetrated at many other points and has come to be a prime element in the industrial expansion of the district.

At Pratt City, should the sight-seer wish to have a lengthy underground journey, he may pass from one slope to another until he has traversed the lower workings of nine inter-communicating mines.

Beyond Pratt City comes Ensley, next in order being Fairfield, through which the great chain of industries, beginning with the Ensley furnace plant and the steel mill, runs without interruption. Beyond Fairfield are found the monumental plants where the steel is rolled that forms the plates in many an ocean vessel; where railroad cars are built in shops so huge that the observer is fairly staggered, and where everything is done upon a scale so large that one marvels at the genius and the courage of those who conceived and executed plans so gigantic.

Further Westward one encounters the great furnace and coke plants of the Woodward Company, and still further is Bessemer, a city separate from Birmingham but connected with two lines of trolley, steam railways, and asphalt and chert highways. Furnaces and pipe plants constitute the chief industries here. Turning back toward Birmingham, one passes a number of ore mines, the huge plant of the Grasselli Chemical Company, and numerous other enterprises of lesser importance.

In addition to the closely grouped industries in the territories referred to, there are two large furnace plants within a half mile of the business section of the city, one on the West and one in the East, and between these lie a great net-work of railroad tracks, traversing the wholesale district. Going East, beyond the Sloss furnaces, one reaches Avondale, where there are a large textile factory, a cotton gin factory, a steel products plant, huge railroad shops, and many other industries.

Verily, the Indian who trailed the deer, the panther and the bear upon these hills and through these vales a little while ago, and who used the red rock (iron ore) to trace gaudy patterns upon his face and limbs, scarcely would recognize his old hunting ground! Instead of the smoke from the tiny tepee, issues the smoke of the giant furnace; instead of the cry of the beast of prey, is the shriek of the deep-throated whistle; instead of the slumbering valley, with the voice of birds and the hum of insects, is the teeming life of a great metropolis.

What a commentary is this upon the intellectual gifts of men; what a tribute to the brain of the Anglo-Saxon!

All of the materials with which the white man wrought this miracle were here when the savage made his way across these hills and valleys. To hunt, to fight, to eat, to sleep, was enough for him.

Then came the white man, eager, ambitious, resourceful, palpitating with the love of conquest, and then the miracle! Under his feet he found the making of an industrial empire, and within his own being he found the strength, the genius and the purpose to transform these raw materials into the finished product.

CHAPTER XXI

FAR-FLUNG INFLUENCES

REFERENCE has been made to the fact that Birmingham is remarkable for the size of its Sunday School classes and for the enthusiasm behind the Sunday School movement. This bald statement may have aroused some curiosity in the minds of readers who are interested in the growth of religious movements, so the answer to the question of how this growth and enthusiasm have been brought about may as well be made a part of the record. It is found in one word — organization.

Sunday School activities in this city are as highly organized as are the operations of the great industrial agencies. Indeed, the same brains that have helped to make many of the last named agencies effective are behind the Sunday School movement, and it is no exaggeration to say that some of the big figures in the industrial and commercial life of the community are more enthusiastic about their Sunday School work than they are about the achievements of the business organizations with which they are connected. This may sound like a fairy tale, but any one who doubts may learn the truth by a little personal investigation. Just interview a few men whom I shall name at random.

Talk with W. H. Stockham, head of a pipe and fitting plant that covers many blocks; A. L. Smith, of the Continental Gin Company; J. A. Vann, or W. M. Franklin, moving spirits in great wholesale enterprises; D. H. Marbury, manufacturer and wholesaler; E. E. Linthicum or C. S. Bissell, industrial leaders, and five minutes' conversation will serve to demonstrate the fact that to them Sunday School work is a business of primary importance. Moreover, it has been put on a business basis through the genius of just such men, aided by the fine spirituality of the many good women identified with the work.

The first step toward the highly specialized organization that exists today was taken back in 1898, when Mrs. William Hardy organized a Primary Sunday School Teachers' Union, the members of which met once a week for the purpose of trying to make more effective the work of instructing children in the primary grades. Gradually the value of co-operative work along these lines so impressed itself upon the community that a demand arose for an extension of the system, and a Junior Department was created, the name of the organization being changed to the Birmingham Graded Union. Later, Intermediate and Adult Departments were added, and the organization became a power in shaping the activities of Sunday Schools throughout the city and district.

The success of this organization in making Sunday School work effective, and in extending its scope, pointed the way for a still more ambitious effort, and there followed the formation of the Birmingham Sunday School Association in 1908, D. H. Marbury and Lee Bonner, two prominent business men, assuming leadership in the movement. Headquarters were opened, a field secretary was employed, the first person to occupy this position being Miss Minnie E. Kennedy, who since has become a nationally known figure in Sunday School work.

The financial support of the organization was made possible by an agreement on the part of the Sunday Schools throughout the district to set aside the collection taken on each fifth Sunday, and, later, by an annual subscription campaign, in which the people at large were asked to contribute. The budget system was adopted, and the work placed upon a practical business basis.

The first Training School was held in 1908, the number of Sunday School teachers and officers, taking the course exceeding two thousand. From that time forward, these Training Schools became annual events, the faculty each year being composed of the most distinguished authorities upon Christian education to be found in the United States, with occasional visitors, of international fame, from lands across the sea. By 1917 the Training School broke the World's record in point of attendance, and Birmingham continues to lead in this phase of work.

The Training School lasts a week, during which time all phases of Christian effort are studied by teachers, officers and field workers, increased efficiency being the key-note.

Membership in the Association is almost universal among Protestant Sunday Schools, and one of the results has been uniformity of effort along the most improved lines. Another result has been to inspire confidence in the Sunday School as a well organized, well equipped and thorough agency in the promotion of Christianity and good citizenship, instead of a hap-hazard, catch-as-catch-can proposition, as too often it was, in the absence of trained leaders, working along well defined lines.

The city is organized by districts, each having a president and each provided with workers who represent the various phases of Sunday School effort. Community Training Schools are held, as are quarterly institutes, all looking forward to the great annual event, and all designed to keep interest and enthusiasm at a high pitch, while increasing efficiency.

But it is not all work with the Sunday School Association. It goes in for pleasure on a big, broad scale. A delightful summer camp is maintained at Winnataska, and there the boys and girls may enjoy a vacation under the leadership of trained men and women, whose duty is to make it a memorable occasion; one profitable physically, mentally and socially. Here the "Camp Fire" girls enjoy their stories of adventure at night, and swim and fish and row by day, while many avenues of clean enjoyment are open to the boys.

Banquets, too, add to the joy of life. "Mothers and Daughters" banquets, and "Fathers and Sons" banquets are regular events of the winter months, and they have been powerful factors in linking the home with the Sunday School.

It would be a mistake to infer that these activities on the part of the Association have served to supplant similar activities in the separate Sunday Schools. These go on, being intensified somewhat by the example of the larger organization, and the historic picnic continues to be an annual event. The difference is that the boys who flock in as the picnic season approaches are more than likely to be held after the fried chicken, the pies and the lemonade had been disposed of. For one of the things the Association teaches is how to grip and to hold the boys and the girls, as well as the older folks, who once find their way into the class room.

Liberality in the support of all denominational undertakings is emphasized, and the type of youngster described by some joke-smith as saying "A fool and his money are soon parted," upon being asked to give a scriptural quotation when dropping his gift into the box, is fast disappearing.

The success of the Sunday School Association idea in Birmingham had the effect of attracting widespread attention, and served to give this city a pre-eminent position. Today organizations framed along similar lines are found in many parts of the country, and training schools, conducted as in Birmingham, are held in many communities.

Another illustration of how a useful idea may

grip the popular imagination and grow at an extraordinary rate is found in the experience of the Civitan Club, of this city, an organization founded upon the idea that business men, by getting together, might render valuable service in the development of community assets.

The first Civitan Club was formed in Birmingham in March, 1917, the organizers having no idea that they were giving expression to an ideal that would seize the popular imagination. Today the Civitan movement has become international, and scarcely a week passes without the organization of a new club somewhere.

Canada and Cuba have been invaded, and at this writing clubs exist in over thirty American cities, the list including Baltimore, Washington, Memphis, New Orleans, Atlanta, Jacksonville, Little Rock, San Antonio, Houston, Dallas, Savannah, Chattanooga, Tulsa, and other widely scattered communities.

The parent organization sprang from a little conference participated in by Dr. C. W. Shropshire, who afterwards became international president, A. C. Crowder, Jelks H. Cabaniss, Dr. C. W. Gewin, Wallace Johns, William Leslie Welton, and one or two others. Dr. Shropshire had suggested that, in his opinion, it would be a good plan for some representative citizens to get together in an organization dedicated to civic betterment, and the meeting was called to discuss the idea. It was then that the initial club was formed, with Arthur Crowder as president.

The first thing to attract the attention of the new-born organization was the fact that thousands of Birmingham men had allowed themselves to become disfranchised through failure to pay their poll tax. Obviously, it was not a healthy state of affairs when so many potential factors in the promotion of improved political conditions occupied this unenviable position. So the Civitan Club launched a campaign of education, stressing the importance of all good citizens becoming qualified voters. The result was to bring about a large increase in poll tax payments, and a quickened appreciation of civic duty.

At the same time steps were taken to throw additional safe-guards about newsboys and others who were forced to work for a livelihood. This led to the promotion of parks and playgrounds, and similar agencies for lightening the tedium of toil, and the results were such as to attract widespread attention. Interest grew and in April, 1920, the International Association of Civitan Clubs was organized in Birmingham, with Dr. Shropshire as president. How the idea has grown, and the scope of the work being undertaken by

LIMESTONE, ORE AND COKE AT FURNACE

the several organizations, may be illustrated by the following: Arkansas recently had a state-wide "Clean-Up" day, inaugurated and directed by the Civitan Clubs of that State; Clubs in Helena and Little Rock, Ark., and in Huntsville, Ala., have caused new parks to be opened to the public; the Atlanta Club recently sponsored and put through a movement for a $200,000 bond issue for a municipal market; the Washington Club is engaged in an effort to obtain increased appropriations for playgrounds in the District of Columbia, and similar activities are reported almost daily to the international headquarters in this city by clubs in various parts of the country.

Another distinction Birmingham enjoys is that of having the second largest Drama League Center in the United States, Chicago, the national headquarters, being the only city having an organization that is stronger numerically. Second place was occupied by Philadelphia until 1920, when, under the leadership of Mrs. John R. Hornady, Mrs. W. D. Smith and other active supporters of the drama, the local center increased its membership to more than nine hundred. New York, it may be observed, by way of explanation, does not maintain membership in the National organization.

Shakespeare came to Birmingham along with

the boomers, and old-timers still chuckle over some of the early performances staged by home talent. For instance, they relate how on one occasion a gentleman who afterward became distinguished in the public life of the community stumbled as he stepped upon the stage, and, as he recovered his balance, but lost his lines, exclaimed, "Where is Cassius at?" and thereby convulsed his audience.

It is a far cry from those days of half-serious, half-hilarious effort toward dramatic interpretation, to the activities of the present, but every step has been marked by progress. The fact that today this city has so many supporters of the dramatic art is one of several surprises awaiting the visitor who comes expecting to find an overgrown mining camp. The world's most distinguished interpreters of the drama are brought here, and invariably they are greeted by large audiences. Nor is this interest in the drama limited to the adult population. There is a Junior League of the local center, with a membership of more than a hundred, and library records show a surprising demand for books upon the subject, and for plays that are in the public eye.

Pageants are a highly popular form of entertainment, and in a district abounding with natural amphitheatres, it is not difficult to find a proper setting for the most elaborate outdoor productions. In many instances these entertainments have hundreds of participants, the last detail of whose preparation and attire has been carefully supervised, and the audiences frequently run into the thousands.

The creation of a musical atmosphere began with the founding of the city, the formation of a band being coincident with the organization of a volunteer fire department. As a matter of fact, the personnel of the fire-fighting aggregation was the same as the music-making contingent in a number of instances, and the two important adjuncts to community life were directed by the same individual. In view of these facts it is not impossible that the familiar phrase, "hot stuff," originated in the mind of some musical critic of that period in an effort to describe the accomplishments of this fire-fighting, note-exploiting company of pioneers.

With the growth of the city the band idea grew, and today practically every important industrial enterprise has its full brass band, made up of employees endowed with musical talent. All the high schools have bands, the city maintains a municipal band, the numerous fraternal bodies have similar organizations, in addition to the regular commercial bands. Add to these the many orchestras to be found about the city, and no further evidence is needed to proclaim Birmingham's devotion to music.

The Music Study Club and the Orchestral Society are two unselfish organizations formed for the purpose of creating a taste for and giving to the public the best in music. The Music Study Club, with a membership of a thousand, has brought to the city many artists of national fame. In this atmosphere of quickened enthusiasm for things musical, a number of artists of exceptional ability have been developed, chief among these being Clara Bridewell, who has won distinction as a grand opera singer. Frederick Gunster, Reed Miller, Bessie Cunningham Sullivan, Charles C. Washburn, Mary Fabian and Bettie Blythe are familiar names in the concert field, and all had their homes in Birmingham at one time or another.

That form of vocal exercise known as the "community sing" has attained widespread popularity in Birmingham, and it is an all-year proposition. During the summer months these "sings" are held in the parks, while in the winter they are held in a theatre provided for that purpose by the city authorities. They attain the height of their popularity during the summer months, and on Sunday afternoons it is not an uncommon thing to find six or eight thousand people gathered in Woodrow Wilson Park to unite their voices in familiar airs. This park, the most central in the city, is provided with an amphitheatre having a seating capacity of eight thousand.

Known for years as Capitol Park, this space was set aside by the bold founders of the city as a site for the State capitol, which they confidently expected to remove from Montgomery, just as they removed the county court house from its ancient moorings in Elyton; but the more the people saw of the State legislature the less inclined they became to have the seat of government removed to this city, and the idea was finally abandoned. However, it was known for years as Capitol Park, the name being changed during the World War as an expression of devotion to Woodrow Wilson. At the same time the name of East Park was changed to Ingram Park, as a memorial to Kelly Ingram, whose bold sacrifice of self during the early stages of the war led the United States Government to name a cruiser in his honor. Behrens Park was, at the same time, changed to Mortimer Jordan Park, in memory of a youthful captain who was killed by a German shell. "The Rainbow Viaduct," that long and beautiful arch of concrete which spans the railroads in the heart of the city, was named in honor of the Rainbow

Division, whose exploits shed lustre upon Alabama.

It was in Woodrow Wilson Park that the boys used to assemble during the war, preparatory to marching for the terminal station, where they boarded long trains for, they knew not where. On these days there was music and speechmaking such as stirred the soul and kindled all the fires of exalted patriotism, and such farewells as wrung the heart and left it numb with loneliness.

On one such occasion, I recall, as the long line swung off for the waiting trains, a slip of a woman, with a baby in her arms, ran up to a strip of a youth and thrust the child into his hands; and I recall how he clasped it to his heart for a moment, without losing step with his comrades, and then passed it back to the little mother, who had moved swiftly at his side. Then he disappeared as the line turned into the station.

I have wondered often what became of the boy, whether he came home, as thousands of others did, and knew again the joy of feeling those baby arms about his neck, or whether he sleeps over there, as other thousands do. And when I think of him, and of the millions like him, who left all that life holds dear, in order that the things we cherish might be preserved, I recall the utterance of the Psalmist who said "If I forget thee, O Jerusalem, may my right hand forget her cunning. If I do not remember thee, let my tongue cleave to the roof of my mouth,'' and feel that some such prayer should be ever in the hearts of our people.

Art as applied to paint and chisel also has found vigorous expression in Birmingham. Moretti resided here for a number of years, being the first to emphasize the value of Alabama marble as a vehicle for expressing the sculptor's art. He declared it to be equal to the best Italian marble — an opinion since confirmed by the wide use to which this marble has been put. This material has been used in ornamenting many of America's most beautiful buildings, and it has gone into numerous works of art.

It was Moretti who made ''Vulcan,'' the colossal statue of iron which was conceived by J. A. McKnight, a newspaper man, and which became the central figure in Birmingham's exhibit at the St. Louis Exposition, attracting as much attention as would have been excited by the Colossus of Rhodes. Brought back from St. Louis, this heroic figure was erected upon the State Fair Grounds, where it stands today, but the suggestion has been made that it be moved to the highest peak on Red Mountain, there to abide permanently. That this will be done is probable, and then Vulcan, the man of iron, will rest upon the mountain of iron from which his component parts were dug nearly a score of years ago.

During the present year some highly creditable paintings by local artists were displayed at the Art Exhibit in Charleston, and visits to local studios reveal a number of canvasses of genuine merit.

Occasional exhibits are held in the Central Library, and systematic effort is made to encourage the art. Patrons are zealous, if not numerous, and while it is somewhat rarefied, Birmingham may be said to have its art atmosphere. J. W. Donnelly, president of the Art League, a man of wealth and exceptional culture, is doing much to promote popular appreciation of the best, and to this end is endeavoring to bring about the creation of an art museum. That such an institution will materialize in time is reasonably certain, but it is too early to discuss architectural details.

CHAPTER XXII

WHETTING THE INTELLECT

CHILDREN were few and far between in Birmingham when the town was first established, and little thought appears to have been given the subject of education, but after a lapse of two years the importance of providing a public school became apparent. By this time, however, the cholera epidemic had come along with its destructive touch, and the municipal treasury was empty. The town did not own a single lot upon which a school building might be erected, and had neither money nor credit.

In this emergency, the man who became the founder of the public school system appeared on the scene in the person of Colonel J. T. Terry. He undertook to raise funds by public subscription, and in this work he received the hearty co-operation of that bluff sea captain, Charles Lynn, who had opened the first bank established here. Colonel Powell, Founder of the City, who had become Mayor, contributed his salary and the fees of his office, and others gave as liberally as possible. The Elyton Land Company donated a site, located at the corner of Sixth Avenue and Twenty-fourth Street, and was thereupon subjected to some criticism because the site was "out in the country," as the critics expressed it, though, as a matter of fact, it was only a few blocks from the heart of the town.

Contributions aggregated about $3,000, and work was started upon what, in those days, was perhaps the most pretentious building in the community, being two stories in height and built of brick. Funds for completing the structure were lacking, and work was suspended for a time, but Colonel Terry came forward again, and loaned the city an amount sufficient to complete the school.

Today, the spirit of Birmingham toward education is best expressed in the program of construction now under way, a program that involves the expenditure of three million dollars within the next few months, and which calls for as much more within the next two or three years.

As this is written one new high school is nearing completion, and another is well under way—

the two to have a combined capacity of twenty-eight hundred children and to represent the most advanced thought in school architecture.

The Central High, with a capacity of two thousand students, occupies a block four hundred feet square, and next year, with its completion, Birmingham will have a High School unsurpassed among structures of its kind. With more than forty class rooms, with an auditorium seating over three thousand persons, with separate gymnasiums for boys and girls, with a completely ap-appointed bank, with complete domestic science and manual training departments, and with every conceivable convenience for the comfort of the pupils, it will proclaim to the world Birmingham's devotion to the welfare of the coming generations, and her high purpose to hold wide the door of opportunity.

A unique feature of this great educational institution is found in the fact that the heating plant, with its smoke and dust, is located on a spur track several hundred feet away. Underground conduits carry the steam from this plant to the school building. An immense warehouse, which also contains the general shops of the Board of Education, stands across the street, between the High School and the heating plant. This arrangement left the architect, D. O. Whilldin, free to design the school building without reference to the heating plant, and the result is apparent in the uniform beauty of the structure.

The next step in the High School program contemplates a new building on the South Side, which will give each of the four great divisions of the city a building convenient to the white students in the several divisions. One immense High School is maintained for the negroes, and here industrial training is emphasized.

While this program of high school erection, involving expenditures which will in the end total something like three million dollars, is going forward, an equally comprehensive plan of betterment in grammar schools is under way. Several magnificent buildings are in course of erection, and a dozen or more additional are being provided for schools that have been outgrown.

In launching this program of school erection, involving millions of dollars, the Board of Education enlisted the co-operation of a group of Birmingham architects, representing the best available home talent, and then called in W. B. Ittner, of St. Louis, as supervising architect. The idea of the Board was not only to have the benefit of the best available talent, but to develop uniformity in construction. The various buildings were assigned to different architects, who were given a comparatively free hand in the matter of decoration and in general arrangement, but were required to hold to certain standards in equipment and materials. As a result, instead of having to carry parts for a dozen different types of heating plants, or for plumbing equipment, the Board of Education will have to carry for the new buildings only one type for repairs and replacements.

Dr. J. H. Phillips, who for years occupied a prominent position among American educators, was Superintendent of the Birmingham schools until his death on July 21, 1921. He came here in 1883, when there was but one school in the community, and served continuously until his death. Today the system embraces sixty schools, with an enrollment of about thirty-five thousand. Emphasis is placed upon the importance of training the hands as well as the mind, and numerous avenues are open to the students for obtaining a working knowledge of useful crafts. In this activity the industrial establishments of the district extend the fullest measure of co-operation, many of them providing means for students to gain practical experience in their establishments.

The strong emphasis placed upon training of this character is due to the fact that Birmingham is fundamentally an industrial community, but school activities are by no means limited to training in the industrial arts. Music and the drama receive the undivided attention of skilled instructors. Two splendid high school bands and two equally efficient orchestras are maintained, and dramatic presentations are numerous. The reserve officers' training corps in the high schools embraces hundreds of students who are under the instruction of regular army officers. Membership is optional, but the military training is popular with the students, and these young men, well drilled and attired in regulation uniforms, make a brave showing when on parade, led by the high school bands.

In the Central High School it has for years been the custom to invite distinguished visitors to address the student body, and the young folks have been privileged to hear addresses by some of the foremost thinkers of the world. This custom resulted in a most amusing incident on one occasion when the speaker proved to have a somewhat limited knowledge of Alabama. He knew that there was a great State University at Tuscaloosa but was unaware that the State Insane Asylum is located in the same community. Therefore, he was unprepared for a gale of uncontrollable laughter which swept the audience when, in closing his address, he exclaimed—"Be faithful in your studies, and, under the wise leadership of Dr.

SCIENCE HALL, BIRMIN HAM SO   ɪE

Phillips and the other distinguished educators here, you will soon be ready for Tuscaloosa!" The howl that went up from the delighted students, whose thoughts turned at once to the asylum, almost swept the speaker off his feet, as he saw nothing at which to be amused, but Dr. Phillips leaned over and whispered to him that the Insane Asylum was at Tuscaloosa, as well as the University. Then the speaker saw the joke and joined in the laughter.

Illiteracy among the whites in Birmingham is practically nil, and, as shown elsewhere in this volume, it is fast disappearing among the negroes.

The impression exists in some quarters that there is a very large foreign population in Birmingham, but this is highly erroneous. As a matter of fact, the 1920 census showed a foreign-born population of only four and three-tenths per cent. Only two schools in the entire city have a considerable number of children of foreign birth, and in these "Americanization" is stressed in such a way that the work of assimilation is thorough.

The Bible is read daily in all the public schools, and while there is no attempt of anything savoring of religious instruction, every effort is made to create high standards of thought and to develop exalted ideals. A creed for Birmingham children was formulated years ago, and every child passing through the schools learns it by frequent repetition. The creed is as follows:

"I am a citizen of Birmingham, of Alabama, and of the United States.

"I will help to make my city a clean, healthful and beautiful place to live in.

"I will help to make my State better by obeying the laws and by helping others to obey them.

"I will be a good American, and will always love my country and my country's flag.

"I will try to learn to make an honest living, so that I may be happy myself and helpful to others.

"I will always try to be fair in play and true in work.

"I will try to be kind to every living thing—the poor, the weak, the old, and especially to dumb animals.

"I pledge these services to my City, my State and my Country."

A loyalty pledge is also required of teachers upon entering the schools, this pledge being one of the products of the war. It reads:

"I am a citizen of the United States of America, and I salute the American flag as the emblem of American Liberty and the symbol of truth and righteous government in the world.

"I pledge to my Country my Love, Obedience

and Loyalty. Love for my Country shall at all times be expressed by words of respect and deeds of service. The laws of my Country shall constitute a claim upon my obedience prior to that of all other laws, no matter by whom enacted or by what authority sanctioned. Loyalty to my Country, its government and its institutions, including the Public Schools, shall have precedence over all lesser loyalties, including those of family or friend, race or nationality, sect or secret society.

"To these fundamental principles of patriotic duty, I fully subscribe, and as a teacher in the public schools, I cheerfully assume the obligation to inculcate the same in the youth placed under my instruction."

The Golden Rule is emphasized in the schools, as is the grace of giving. A Thanksgiving offering is taken each year in all the schools, the money going to various charities, and Red Cross seals are purchased by the children at every Christmas season. During the war, large sales of war-saving stamps were made through the schools, and all the calls for money to aid war agencies met a ready response. Indeed, there is nothing more beautiful in the school system than the enthusiasm with which the children respond when appealed to in behalf of a worthy cause.

Another striking feature about the public

schools is the interest shown by parents in school conditions. Every elementary school has its improvement association, composed of the mothers of the community, and they carry on a highly constructive work. They have charge of the lunch room, which is a feature of practically all schools, and also give close attention to playgrounds and recreational equipment. As a result, practically all schools have well equipped playgrounds upon which the body is developed while the mind is off its studies.

In several of the larger schools the "work-study-play" system, new in its application to the American public schools, has been adopted. Its universal application is made impossible by reason of the fact that a number of the older school buildings are without auditoriums, which are essential to the application of the system.

The chief advantage of the plan consists in the fact that each class room may be used by two classes of pupils daily, instead of one class. The school is divided into two sections of approximately equal numbers; while one section is engaged in the usual class recitations, the other section is engaged in study halls, auditorium exercises, music, shopwork, home economics, play and physical training, science, laboratory, etc. While saving in class room space, the plan requires more teachers and more equipment. "One of the incidental advantages," Dr. Phillips once remarked, "is the breaking up of traditional lines and giving more flexibility and interest to the work. But its successful operation in any school depends, very largely, upon the principal's initiative and power of leadership."

A modern innovation in the schools is a system under which credits are given for work in the Sunday Schools of the city. Blanks are provided upon which Sunday School Superintendents and teachers report, and when these reports come up to the standards required in the schools, credit is given just as upon work in the class-room.

The health of the children is safeguarded through a system of medical inspection, directed by Dr. James S. McLester, who is assisted by an efficient corps of trained nurses. Teachers who observe any indication of physical impairment of a child file a report with the principal, who turns it over to the medical inspector, and thereupon a thorough examination is made and the parents are advised what to do. By this means the handicap of many children is removed. During the past years 385 cases of enlarged tonsils and adenoids were discovered and corrected, while 65 children with defective vision received attention. Many other ills, the indications of which were so slight as to pass unnoticed by parents, were detected and the children given proper attention. The care of the body is strongly emphasized and a great constructive work is carried on throughout this department.

A well trained mind, a sound body, a knowledge of how to put the hands to useful tasks, reverence for things spiritual, love of country, and of fellows, and a proper appreciation of the rights of others — these are the ideals for which the educational forces of Birmingham stand, and their achievements form a luminous chapter in the history of the community.

Two denominational colleges are located in Birmingham, one maintained by the Baptists, and the other by the Methodists, and they are growing and virile institutions. There are also a number of private schools that enjoy an enviable reputation, and three large business colleges that draw students from a wide territory. The oldest of these, the Wheeler Business College, stands in the very heart of the city, and out of it, as out of the others, there flows an endless stream of young men and young women, eager to join in the pulsing life about them. The impression that Birmingham offers rare opportunities to the young and purposeful has the effect of drawing hundreds of students to the city, and most of them graduate into the industrial and commercial life of the district.

In a community where trained minds are in demand, and where technical knowledge is so essential, it is surprising that there exists no great institutions specializing along these lines. But such is the case. However, it is only a question of time when the splendid work being done along these lines in the high schools will eventuate in the founding of such an institution as a part of the public school system. Classes from the Georgia Tech, from Auburn and from similar institutions are brought to Birmingham at frequent intervals that the students may see the practical application of the knowledge they are acquiring. These students are shown through the great industrial establishments of the district, and are stimulated by actual contact with the work for which they are being prepared.

CHAPTER XXIII

A CITY OF EX-EXECUTIVES

IN addition to its other distinctions, Birmingham might aptly be termed a city of ex-executives. This city does not name many governors, but it claims many, for it has become the habit of men upon leaving the State Capitol in Montgomery forthwith to move to this community.

William Dorsey Jelks, who astonished the politicians by leaving a large balance in the State treasury; Emmet O'Neal, under whose administration the saloons came back for a brief farewell performance, and B. B. Comer, who spent four strenuous years in an effort to tame the railroads of the State, all have their homes here, and two other ex-Governors, Cobb and Cunningham, resided here during their declining years. N. L.

Miller, the present Lieutenant Governor, has his home here, and the Governor of today, Thomas Kilby, has large manufacturing interests in this community. This also is the home of Frank S. White, former United States Senator, and of Frank P. Glass, who came within one vote of being a member of what the members are fond of calling "the greatest deliberative body on earth."

The experience of Frank Glass, who until recently was president of the American Newspaper Publishers' Association, forms one of the most unique chapters in the history of Alabama politics. He was the second editor of the Birmingham News who seemed destined to the Senate, but who failed by reason of an extraordinary chain of circumstances. The story of how Rufus N. Rhodes was kept out of that august body by means of the famous "post-mortem" primary has been told. How Glass, who succeeded Rhodes as editor of the News, upon the death of the former, was defeated is an equally interesting story.

Glass had been a vigorous supporter of the policies of Governor Emmet O'Neal, and when Senator Joseph F. Johnston died, O'Neal named Glass, intending that he should serve until an election could be held for the choice of a successor.

The activities of Glass in opposition to prohibition won for him the cordial opposition of the "dry" element, both in Alabama and in the nation at large, and when he went to Washington for the purpose of taking his seat a terrific fight was waged to prevent the confirmation of the appointment, this fight being carried to the floor of the Senate.

Glass and Woodrow Wilson had been on intimate terms for years, and the President threw all the weight of his influence behind his old-time friend when the fight opened. The anti-prohibitionists also took up the issue when the prohibitionists became active, and the fight waged right merrily, Glass, in the meantime, being given the privileges of the floor of the Senate. Several leading Republicans among the "antis" came over to Glass, and there is no doubt that he had a majority at one time, but the fight drifted finally into a partisan affair, and some Republicans fell away, with the result that when the ballot was taken Glass lacked just one vote of becoming a United States Senator. The point raised against him was that the Governor did not have the authority to make a recess appointment, but the thing that beat him was his uncompromising fight against prohibition in his home State. But for the bitter and prolonged fight made upon him by the enemies he won because of this issue, undoubtedly he would have been seated weeks before the time when partisanship, as between Democrats and Republicans, arose to complicate the affair.

Oddly enough, when viewed by the results in the Glass case, Alabama elected an anti-prohibitionist when a permanent successor to Senator Johnston was chosen. Oscar W. Underwood, who had represented the Ninth Alabama District for a quarter of a century, and had become the author of the Underwood Tariff Act, was the gentleman chosen, this after a most spectacular fight between him and Captain Richmond Pearson Hobson, whose exploit with the Merrimac was then fresh in the public mind. The prohibition issue was drawn then, as in the campaign when Underwood sought re-election, but, while the dominant sentiment in the State was "dry," thousands of prohibitionists supported Underwood and he won handsomely. The same issue was raised six years later when he sought to succeed himself, but again it was unavailing.

The opponent of Senator Underwood in his second race was L. Breckenridge Musgrove, who, as Chairman of the Ratification Committee of the Anti-Saloon League of America, led the successful fight for the adoption of the Eighteenth Amendment. Though Musgrove was fresh from his triumph in the fight for a dry America when he took up the gauge of battle against Underwood, the latter received a majority over both his opponents, Judge Samuel D. Weakley, another prohibitionist, being in the race also.

Judge Weakley, the third man in this spectacular contest, was the author of Alabama's prohibition laws — the most drastic ever drawn at the time of their adoption. These laws, involving many new departures, were upheld when tested in the Supreme Court of the State, and, thereafter, Judge Weakley was called upon to assist in the preparation of similar laws in other Southern States, where it was the purpose to clamp the lid on as tight as possible. It was because of his prominence in this connection that he offered for the Senate against Underwood, and in competition with Musgrove, and the fact that he ran far behind Musgrove was a great disappointment to him. An outstanding figure in the prohibition movement, he expected united prohibition support, and when he fell far short of his ambition, and saw an anti-prohibitionist returned to the Senate with the aid of thousands of prohibition votes, he was never quite the same, and died about a year later.

A man of remarkable industry and uncompromising in his attitude toward the liquor traffic, Judge Weakley spent the last ten or twelve years of his life in trying to evolve new and more stringent measures for killing the business, and for keeping it dead. It was he who originated the idea that property connected with the illegal sale or manufacture of liquor should be confiscated — a law that is on the statute books today, and under which many liquor runners have lost their automobiles. It was this law which added piquancy to the news, flashed over the country some two or three years ago, that a moonshine still had been discovered upon the Alabama farm of Dr. Pearly Baker, President of the National Anti-Saloon League. The question, "Will the good doctor lose his farm?" was the subject of considerable debate, some of the contributions being of ribald character. As a matter of course, everybody knew that Dr. Baker was ignorant of the presence of the illicit still, and many believed it to have been a "plant," designed to cause him embarrassment. At any rate, he took the incident good naturedly and nothing ever came of it. He still owns the farm and spends much of his time in this State.

Another law that is peculiar to Alabama, and for which Judge Weakley was responsible, is one under which is prohibited the sale of any beverage that looks like, tastes like or bears any of the earmarks of intoxicating liquors. Thus all those non-alcoholic drinks being turned out by the brewing companies are outlawed in this State. In this connection I recall an incident that occurred one

Summer day while I was driving through the country to Montgomery, with a party of gentlemen who were interested in certain matters pending before the State Legislature. When we reached a small town about thirty miles out of Birmingham, I told the negro chauffeur to stop at a drug store so that we might get something refreshing to drink. As we got out of the car and started to the store, the negro said, "I's gwin' to get me a bottle of beer while you gentlemen's in there." I paid no attention to him, but went on into the drug store. Stopping in front of the soda fountain I turned to ask my companions what they would have, and not a man was in sight. Going to the door, I glanced down the street and saw the whole crowd following the darky! What they got, as I learned later, was a drink of that brew which some wit described as looking like beer, foaming like beer and tasting like beer, but not having any "authority."

I have seen these imitation beers sold in several other small towns over the State, but the law with reference to their sale is enforced strictly in most communities, as it is in Birmingham. The theory upon which this law is based is that to legalize the sale of a thing that looks so real is to open the way for the handling of that which is real. So every effort to place these "soft" drinks within the law in Alabama has failed. The fact that they have no "kick" has not minimized the kick against their sale.

Meanwhile, there has been a tremendous development in what is termed the legitimate "soft drink" business. I have in mind one wholesale grocery house in this city which began the manufacture of a ginger ale, which, for some reason, is called "Buffalo Rock," and now the soft drink end of the business has come to overshadow the grocery end. "Colas" of every imaginable kind have come upon the market and the plants producing them have attained large proportions. This line of drinks had its beginning with Coco-Cola, a preparation the manufacture of which has become a colossal industry in the South, plants existing in practically every city of importance. Then there is Chero-Cola, which has also become the basis of large industries in Birmingham and elsewhere, and others too numerous to recall.

These and similar preparations flow in a vast endless stream, and in these days of aridity, when one is invited to "have a drink," it usually means to have something of this kind set before him. These cola drinks usually are referred to as "dope," and not infrequently one hears an order for "a shot in the arm." This is interpreted by the clerk to mean the same thing as "dope."

Should one infer from these familiar references that these cola drinks possess some lethal quality, it would be to fall into error. The pioneer manufacturer was subject to unsuccessful attack by the Federal Government in the early days of the enterprise, and this litigation no doubt had the effect of creating in the public mind the impression that there was some extraordinary quality about the product. Out of this grew the term "dope," and once this term came into common use, it took the versatile American only a little while to convert it into "a shot in the arm."

Along with the enormous consumption of drinks such as have been described, came a corresponding increase in the demand for fruit drinks, and for "ice-cream soda," as well as ice-cream. In fact, there is nothing more striking than the growth of the ice-cream industry since the passing of the saloons. Plants have multiplied in a surprising manner, and as a rule old establishments have had to greatly enlarge their facilities. Ice-cream "parlors" have multiplied, too, and many of these are fitted up upon a scale of elegance that is equal to that which characterized the most fashionable saloons before those institutions became so unfashionable. Incidentally, it is interesting to visit one of these places and to note, as one can on frequent occasions, how once familiar patrons of

TWO VIEWS FROM THE SKY. TERMINAL STATION
IN CENTER OF LOWER PICTURE

the bar have learned to wield an ice-cream spoon with as much skill as that displayed by the popular society girl, and to imbibe their "dope" or "soda" without once attempting to blow the foam off the top.

In the consumption of ice-cream, many of these lads who once kept the cash register in the saloons busy, find their favorite form of "dissipation" today. They also have brought about a considerable increase in the consumption of candies, particularly of chocolates, and the manufacturers of these confections are reaping at least a part of the wealth that once flowed into the coffers of the brewers and distillers.

The dairyman, too, is a beneficiary of the altered condition. He furnishes the principal ingredients for ice-cream and "soda," and is called upon to supply a largely increased volume of buttermilk, for this product of the dairy has become as popular with many ordinary citizens as once it was reputed to be with Vice-President Fairbanks. The impression that the Vice-President was passionately fond of buttermilk, which impression caused him to be confronted with it on practically all occasions when he was being entertained, was one of the results of his fondness, not so much for milk, as for his buttermilk joke. This joke, which doubtless is familiar to most people who had attained the voting age when Mr. Fairbanks became Vice-President, caused an unexpected laugh, and no little embarrassment, to a prominent office-holder in this city, at a dinner being given the Vice-President.

The story, as I recall it, concerned three gentlemen who were much given to the flowing bowl. They drank industriously for many years, and no rift arose to threaten their friendship. Then suddenly two of them reformed. The third, not knowing of the sudden reformation, met the two and extended the usual invitation. When the trio lined up at the bar and the white-aproned attendant asked "What will it be?" one of the reformed men said, "I'll take a ginger-ale," while the other said "Give me a glass of buttermilk." Turning upon the pair with a savage scowl, and throwing the maximum of sarcasm into his tones, the unregenerated one exclaimed, "Give me a piece of pumpkin pie!"

When the Vice-President told this oft-repeated tale, most of those about the board smiled their appreciation, but the local office-holder threw his head back and laughed uproariously, making so much noise that Mr. Fairbanks turned to him, with a bright and hopeful look upon his face, and asked, "Did you never hear that one before?"

The local office-holder was a churchman and a

conscientious man, and though he would have given much to have left the honored guest under the impression that he had one auditor to whom his favorite joke was new, he couldn't bring himself to lie about it. So, blushing to the roots of his hair, he stammered:

"Well, I-I-I never heard it but-but once!"

The laugh that followed almost raised the roof, and the local office-holder did not hear the end of it for years.

Another laugh that was not in the regular order added to the gaiety of a meeting here some years ago when the speaker was John Allen, the once famous Congressman from Mississippi, who won national fame as a wit by saying in a speech, made shortly after his arrival on the floor at Washington, that he was the only private in the Confederate Army, and who thenceforward was known as "Private John." The speaker told a number of his inimitable jokes and then, speaking in a serious vein, he began to recite the wonderful gifts of Mississippi to Birmingham. He told of numerous citizens of prominence who had moved from the Delta State into this city and had played an active part in the upbuilding of the community, concluding with the declaration "and, most conspicuous of all, we gave you Senator Frank S. White."

Before the audience had time to express its appreciation of this "gift," by the usual applause, some one in the rear, with a high-pitched and penetrating voice, cried out:—"Well, we've done forgive you for that; let by-gones be by-gones!"

Senator White, who was seated on the stage at the time, enjoyed the laugh which followed as much as any of those present.

Southern orators frequently are famous for their jokes, and Birmingham, with its numerous ex-governors, ex-senators, etc., hears much of this sort of thing, but one of the exceptions to the rule is Oscar Underwood. I have heard him speak on many occasions, but do not recall an instance in which he paused to say "and that reminds me," which is the unvarying prelude of a funny story. Senator Tom Heflin, on the other hand, is one of the most noted story tellers in Alabama, and his fund of yarns would fill a volume. He went to the House of Representatives upon waves of laughter, for term after term, and when a vacancy arose in the Senate, he created a tidal-wave, and was swept into that dignified body amid the sound of merriment.

One of his stories, which was new to me, had to do with the experience of a man whose thirst was accentuated by the absence of that with which to quench it. Determined to obtain liquor in some way, he went to a physician and pretended to be ill, but the scheme did not work, the physician, according to Heflin, saying "The only thing I can give you liquor for is to counteract the poison of snake-bite." Thereupon the thirsty one hastened away, only to reappear early the next morning in a most disheveled condition. "What in the world is the matter with you?" asked the physician, as he contemplated the torn condition of the man's clothing, and the scratches which appeared on his hands and face.

"I spent the night wandering around in the swamp," was the reply.

"What did you do that for?"

"Why, I was trying to get bit by a snake," replied the thirsty one.

"Did you succeed?"

"No," was the reply, uttered in a tone of deep disgust. "Every snake in that swamp is dated up for the next six weeks."

Most of the stories of the Southern statesmen and politicians have to do with the eccentricities of the negro, a fair sample being this one, told by W. D. Nesbitt, Chairman of the State Democratic Executive Committee — and perhaps by many others:

A darky who had buried two wives and who had called upon a bosom friend to act as one of the pall-bearers upon each occasion, finally suffered the loss of a third, and, as was his custom, he called on the friend to act as pall-bearer.

"No, sah," answered the friend, "I ain't gwin' to serve in no such capa-city no mo'."

"You ain't!" exclaimed the bereaved one. "You's always acted for me befo' an' I was a countin' on you."

"Tain't no use a countin' on me," was the reply, "cause I ain't gwin' do it no mo'."

"Why is you done come to that 'cision?"

"Cause I's made up my min' I ain't gwin' to accept no more favors what I can't return."

Another famous story teller is Hugh Morrow, who has presided at the head of miles and miles of dinner tables, and who doubtless holds the record for saying "We have with us this evening," since he is the recognized toastmaster of the community. One of his characteristic stories, told as illustrative of how hot it becomes in a certain rural community, concerns a rabbit hunt, which, ordinarily, is not without some element of excitement.

"I saw a hound chasing a rabbit," he said, "and both of them were walking!"

This he construed as the *ne plus ultra* of inertia.

It has been said that a good Democrat seldom dies and never resigns, but Birmingham has an ex-Congressman who resigned in order to make his home in this city. S. J. Bowie, who represented the Fourth District of Alabama for a number of years, quit to take up his residence here. As this is written he is acting as Chairman of the Semi-Centennial Committee, which is arranging an elaborate celebration in observance of the fiftieth birthday of Birmingham.

The first act of this Committee was to gain the consent of President Harding to be the guest of honor during Semi-Centennial week, and by the time these lines appear the President will have made his first visit to Birmingham, and delivered his first address in the South since his inauguration.

The "ex" is not monopolized by the men of Birmingham, as one might infer from the foregoing. Mrs. Solon Jacobs is an ex-National Committeeman — or woman — of the Democratic persuasion. Mrs. James A. Going, Mrs. C. P. Orr, Mrs. Joseph McLester and Mrs. L. J. Haley are ex-Presidents of the State Federation of Women's Clubs. Mrs. Haley is now a Director of the National Federation of Women's Clubs. Mrs. Bossie O'Brien Hundley is ex-President of the State Federation of Music Clubs, as is Mrs. Victor H. Hanson. Mrs. Chappell Cory is ex-President of the Alabama Women's Christian Temperance

Union, an organization which supplied most of the energy for bringing about prohibition in the State.

Alabama's woman representative on the Democratic National Committee at this time is Mrs. John D. McNeel, wife of the Collector of Internal Revenue. How long the husband of a Democratic National Committeeman will hold a job under a Republican Administration is a matter of speculation. He, too, may have joined the "Ex" club before this volume appears. In this connection, there is an element of irony in the fact that a group of Republicans shortly will be occupying the magnificent new Government building, erected here by a Democratic Administration with the devout hope that it would continue to house the followers of Jefferson.

Incidentally, this splendid marble building, though just completed, even now is too small for the needs of Birmingham, and it furnishes another illustration of the difficulty experienced in providing for the future. Nearly every building put up here is outgrown before its completion. Some time ago two new high schools were started, to have a combined capacity of two thousand eight hundred children. In the meantime, the attendance in the group of old buildings that are being replaced has gone beyond three thousand. This means that another new building is needed before the completion of the two that were expected to meet the situation. As Sid Bowie once observed while a member of the Board of Education, "The child factory in Birmingham never shuts down," and he might have added that the demands of the adult population seem ever to elude the efforts of those whose business it is to anticipate the needs of tomorrow.

CHAPTER XXIV

THE SNAKE-CHARMER ECLIPSED

IT was noon-time in the great wire mill, and the heads of departments were gathered around five long tables in the dining room upon the second floor of the office building. The appointments and the service were such as one would expect to find in a first-class hotel, while the atmosphere was that of an intimate sort of social club. Through the windows could be seen the tennis courts and the athletic field, while in the distance the mountains stood out clear and green in the Summer sun.

Conversation buzzed at all the tables, hunting being the theme at the one where I sat. "I found that there is a lot of horse-play about the hunting proposition the last time I went," said the man to my right. "A party of us were at a resort in Wisconsin in search of deer, and the men we had as guides and mentors put us through all the motions that we had read about. They made the stalking of this particular game as mysterious and as romantic as they could, and fulfilled all our preconceived notions about the precautions one had to take if success was to be achieved. Under their directions we went great distances, and waited long hours in deep and silent forest retreats, and had all sorts of thrills. The result was that when we did land a deer, we felt like the victors in a thrilling battle; the wearisome marches and the long waits seemed eminently worth while. But, gee, how good it felt to get back in camp after one of those hard days!

"Everything would have been lovely but for the fact that we were disillusioned just as we were preparing to break camp. That afternoon those two guides picked up a shot-gun apiece and walked away from the camp. In about sixty minutes they were back, each having killed a deer! Gradually we learned, through the disingenuous conversation of these guides, that deer were plentiful in that vicinity, and that the long and toilsome tramps through which we had gone meant only that the guides wanted to give us our money's worth. They reasoned, rightfully, no doubt, that had we been shown how to go out a mile or two from camp and kill a deer within an hour, the entertainment soon would have palled, which is about the last thing a guide wants to happen."

Others contributed brief experiences or observations, and the conversation waxed merrily, until suddenly the superintendent picked up a small gavel that rested by his plate, and gave the table a rap. Thereupon every man in the room pushed his chair back against the wall, and there was silence. Then, in short, crisp sentences, man after man made a report concerning the conditions of his department. This done, the gavel fell again, and all hands were away to their posts. The transition from pleasure to business was instantaneous, and thus was given a fine illustration of the line of cleavage drawn in such establishments. When it is in order to have a pleasant hour, then one is expected to enjoy himself to the full. When it is time for work, then every man is expected to be on the job, as the saying is, and to see that the maximum of results is obtained.

This plant of the American Steel & Wire Company, a subsidiary of the Steel Corporation, is one of the most spectacular performers in the Birmingham district, and is one of the largest as well as the most modern of its kind in America. In its so-called "roughing mill," one may witness such serpentine performances as no snake charmer ever dreamed of. Billets, fifty inches long and four inches square, come to this plant from the neighboring steel mill, and are lifted from the cars by large magnets, being deposited upon "skids." Sliding along these "skids," the billets pass into a furnace, from which they drop, white-hot, into a trough through which they are skidded up to the rolls.

The rolls seize these hot slabs of steel and quickly reduce them to rods, which increase in length and decrease in size at a most amazing rate. Presently the glowing bar of fifty inches has become a crimson streak of a hundred yards or more, and as these hurrying rods perform their weird contortions, they are kept in bounds by men with hooks and thongs, who are ever on the jump.

These rushing, squirming rods of red hot steel are reduced to three-fourths of an inch in the roughing mill, and, still hot, they are directed into another mill, where they become almost as small as the wire that is strung on telegraph poles. The machine that reduces the rod to this size delivers it coiled and tied, in which form it is ready for treatment, preparatory to being worked into nails, tacks, barbed wire, plain wire, woven fencing, or any other of the products flowing from this plant.

The operation, from the moment when the fifty-inch billet enters the rolls, until the huge coil is formed, is continuous. Now comes a récess. The steel, in passing through the rolls, has accumulated a "scale" that must be removed before the rods are passed through the "dies," and are thus reduced to wire of varying sizes. First, they are given an acid treatment, followed by a shower of water, which continues until they are covered with rust. Then they are covered with lime and placed in an oven, where they are allowed to remain and bake for several hours.

Coming from the oven, the coils are taken to the wire department, where they are drawn to the various sizes. Nails such as are required for bridge building are made of wire that is nearly as large as a pencil. Nails used in cabinet work may be made from wire no larger than the lead in a pencil. These varying sizes are obtained by drawing the steel through a series of holes, each being a bit smaller than the other, and each shaped somewhat like a funnel.

In the nail department great batteries of machines turn out all sizes and shapes amid a perfect inferno of noise. Here the sign language is used exclusively, the vocal chords having no chance in a contest with those steel-lipped monsters. The wire is fed into these machines from a coil, and at the other end nails clatter down like corn from a sheller.

These nails are packed in kegs of one hundred pounds each, and it is interesting to watch the operation of the highly intelligent machine which does the packing. As the nails rain down from the hopper, the machine shakes the kegs vigorously, and, at the exact moment when the weight becomes a hundred pounds, it raises a warning hand, so to speak, and the flow stops until another empty keg slides into place.

As the kegs are filled, they move on a conveyor, receiving the top and certain additional fasteners as they go forward, and presently are in the warehouse, where the weight is verified. Then they are ready to catch the next barge for the Gulf, or to go into the buildings being erected in the ever-growing city of Birmingham. These kegs, by the way, are made next door in a cooperage shop, where most of the operations are automatic.

But the most amazing part of this establishment is where they make the wire fencing. How these big machines manage to take spools of wire and weave them into beautiful fence patterns is difficult to explain, and I shall not attempt it. They turn out roll after roll of different sizes and different patterns, and make a thorough but noisy job of it. Barbed wire also is made in the same room, though the barbs are not so long nor so sharp as when the great spools were being sent to France and Belgium to form entanglements for the Germans.

All of the wire entering into the fence making department is galvanized, a process that involves heating the wire, passing it through an acid bath, and, finally, through a zinc bath. Large quantities of acid are used, and the final use to which this acid is put forms an interesting story in itself. When the acid has lost its efficiency in the plant, it is conveyed to great vats, where all sorts of iron and steel junk is thrown into it. The weak acid, working on this metal, finally exhausts every atom of energy, and then is ready for the production of sugar sulphate of iron. This chemical is used very widely in the purification of water, the output being absorbed in large part by cities throughout the South. It also has numerous other uses.

Recreational features are emphasized strongly by this great manufacturing enterprise. There is a band of fifty pieces, which gives periodic concerts at noon-time, furnishes music for sundry events in neighboring communities, and plays in public parks from time to time. A baseball team is maintained, having membership in the league operated within the Tennessee organization, and there are numerous other forms of entertainment and recreation.

There is an emergency hospital, a physician and a corps of nurses, and the big hospital of the Tennessee Company is available for the ill or injured. Extraordinary precautions are taken to prevent accidents, three-fold measures being provided for stopping the machinery in the event some one gets caught in the wire, or is otherwise imperiled.

There is a warehouse a thousand and eighty feet long, a pattern room, where is stored a pattern of every piece of machinery in the plant, and an immense machine shop, where parts may be repaired or made, whenever breaks occur.

As in other like industries, the water consumption is enormous, and elaborate provision is made for conserving the supply. After being once used, it is caught in a great pump, and then is purified, filtered and made ready for further use. In this way about eighty percent of the fluid is saved.

In a community where millions of gallons of water are consumed hourly, an adequate source of supply is essential to growth, and Birmingham is fortunate in that it possesses abundant resources along this line. For its own industrial purposes, the Tennessee Company built an impounding reservoir that is enormous in extent and from which flows normally from sixty to seventy million gallons per day.

The regular water supply of Birmingham is obtained from two sources, the chief source being the Cahaba River, where a great dam was erected, forming "Lake Purdy." The water is beautifully clear and, when it reaches the consumer, is absolutely pure. In fact, the excellence of Birmingham's water supply constitutes one of the prime assets of the city.

In designing a water works system for Birmingham, the pioneers displayed again that boundless faith which is made manifest in so many directions. The initial plant, upon Village Creek, was started about a year after the incorporation of the city, and was completed in 1873, the reservoir having a capacity of 1,000,000 gallons. This supply was far in excess of the needs of the hour, as the people seemed to prefer well water, or to purchase it by the barrel when hauled in from nearby springs.

Like the early furnaces, this water works system developed into a white elephant, and the builders, the Elyton Land Company, finally agreed to turn the enterprise over, lock, stock and barrel, to Travers Daniel, provided he would operate it. Daniel, visioning a life of ease as the head of a great public utility, seized upon the offer, and

CIVIC CENTRE, FAIRFIELD

took full charge of the enterprise. However, the first year had not run its course before he sent word to the owners that at the close of the twelve-months period they would "have to feed their own elephant," and Daniel stepped from under on December 31, 1874. Major W. J. Milner, secretary of the company, was then made superintendent of the water plant, and he held this position continuously for a quarter of a century, building, in the meantime, the nucleus of the magnificent system that is in existence in this city today.

With the growth of the community, there finally arose a real demand for water, and it became necessary to enlarge the system. In acquiring additional land for water-sheds, it became necessary to obtain a small portion of a 480-acre farm, the owner of which thought he saw an opportunity to dispose of his place at a fancy figure. To this end he refused to sell any part of the property unless the farm was purchased outright, and his price was $10,000. The company felt that it was being imposed upon, but it had to have the property, and finally paid $9,900 for it. Later a quarry was opened on this farm, there being an unusually fine deposit of limestone thereon, and the amount realized from this quarry was many times the purchase price of the entire property.

The farmer had unloaded a veritable mint upon an unwilling purchaser.

While plans for the liberal extension of the original water works system were under way, and work on a large dam actually was in progress, the growth of the city increased with such rapidity that the necessity of finding a new source of supply, capable of much larger development, became obvious. Therefore, work upon the proposed 30-foot dam, which was to impound the waters of Village Creek, was stopped, and the development of the present system began upon the Cahaba River. Then, instead of a reservoir of one million gallons, there was provided a reservoir of over one hundred and twenty-five million gallons. Moreover, abundant provision was made for future extensions, the result being that, that by this foresighted policy, Birmingham's water problem was solved for many years to come. The reservoir today has a capacity of 1,500,000,000 gallons.

The new system was completed in 1891, since which time there have been periodic enlargements, until today it serves some 300,000 people. At this writing, about $500,000 is being expended in improvements, the larger portion going into duplicate pumping machinery. The water is carried from the reservoir to the filtration plant, from whence it is piped to the city through a tunnel that pierces Red Mountain.

Originally the property of the land company that founded Birmingham, the system has been owned for over thirty years by the Birmingham Water Works Company. A new contract, covering a period of thirty years, recently was entered into between the company and the city, under which the municipality was given an option to buy at any time upon giving six months' notice of its intentions so to do, the purchase price to be $8,000,000, or $3,000,000 under the valuation placed upon the plant by the engineers of the Public Utilities Commission of the State.

The fact that a supply of water sufficient to meet the needs of a city of nearly a million people should have been tapped at a time when Birmingham had a population of less than twenty thousand, furnishes another striking illustration of the fact that the founders of the city had boundless faith in its future.

The dam erected to impound the waters of the Cahaba created a large and beautiful lake about twelve miles from Birmingham, and it furnishes one of numerous fishing resorts about the city. Stocked years ago with bass, brim and perch, it affords fine sport when the fish are disposed to bite. But before one can enjoy this sport, he must have a permit from Harry Horner, the Superintendent, and sometimes I suspect that Harry has a system of tipping the fish off about when to bite and when not to bite, for they act in a most eccentric manner, leaping joyously at the bait upon some occasions, and, on others, ignoring it with cold and studied indifference.

There is another large artificial lake near Birmingham where those who fancy gold fish might enjoy themselves, granting the management would consent. It was the intention to stock this lake with bass, and the large shipment of tiny fish that went into the waters was supposed to be bass, but the wires had been crossed somewhere, for that lake is stocked today with gold fish, tens of thousands of them, and when a "school" passes along it looks like a streak of burnished brass. But catching gold fish isn't much sport at best, save for the cat that attempts to get one from the bowl on the center table, and few applications are made to fish in these waters.

In addition to developing Birmingham's splendid water supply, and developing the city's most beautiful thoroughfare along Red Mountain, Major Milner conceived and caused to be built the Birmingham Belt Railroad, which links the city with many of the most important enterprises in the district. A slender man, under the average height, and as gentle as a woman, he was gifted with extraordinary vision, and with unusual capacity for translating visions into realities. He died early in 1921, having lived to see Birmingham grow from nothing into the third city in the South in point of population, and second to none in its potentialities.

Major Milner and his elder brother, John T., were Southern to the core, and were proud of the fact that to Southerners was due the major credit for building the South's great industrial center. John T. was especially vigorous upon the subject, and the only rebuke I ever heard of his giving his younger brother was once, many years ago, when he learned that Willis J. was reading "Uncle Tom's Cabin." "Burn the —— thing up" was the injunction of John T., and thereupon one copy of the famous war story passed out of circulation.

Another veteran of the War of '61-65, who had a conspicuous part in the development of Birmingham during the last quarter of a century, was Major E. M. Titwiler, who belonged to that immortal body of youngsters from the Virginia Military Institute who, in 1864, joined the army of General John C. Breckenridge, and a few days later achieved the amazing victory at New Market; a victory for which those boys were thanked upon the field of battle by Colonel Patton, acting under the instructions of General Breckenridge, and following which they were called to Richmond, there to be reviewed by President Davis and Governor Smith, and thanked by the Confederate Congress.

In speaking of this exploit, Major Tutwiler tells of the precipitate flight of a number of negroes who were just entering New Market when the battle commenced, and in this connection he says that this would have suited the father of Polk Miller to a "T." It was the father of Polk who, on the eve of the battle of Manassas, sent his son a letter reading in this wise:

"Dear Polk: I hear that you are likely to have a big battle soon, and I write to tell you not to let Sam go into the fight with you. Keep him well in the rear, for that negro is worth $1,000."

Capt. Alberto Martin, after whom the Martin School is named, was another valiant soldier of the Confederacy who helped to guide the infant city through the shoals. It was he who furnished the legal assistance necessary to defeat the plans of those who attempted to obtain sole possession of the site of the proposed city, and he also was conspicuous, as a member of the State Legislature, in bringing about the means of escape from "carpet-bag" government.

Another veteran who wore the gray was Colonel E. W. Rucker, conspicuous in the early history of the city. General Rucker was wounded and taken prisoner at the battle of Nashville in 1864, and was the recipient of unusual courtesies at the hands of his captors. He was carried to the headquarters of General Winston, where Colonel Hatch, of General Winston's staff, gave up his own bed to the wounded Confederate, sleeping on the floor by the side of General Rucker and showing him every attention possible. Though he lost an arm at this time, General Rucker became a two-fisted fighter in the struggle to put Birmingham on the map.

Joseph F. Johnston, who afterward became Governor of Alabama, and then went to the United States Senate, was another of the veteran group, as was Capt. Frank S. White, who followed Johnston in the Senate. Another was Capt. Ben F. Roden, founder of the town of Avondale, builder of the first gas works in Birmingham, and a conspicuous figure in the financial life of the community in the early days. Henry F. DeBardeleben, builder of furnaces and developer of mines, and founder of the city of Bessemer, also was a Confederate veteran, and there were many others who threw into the work of city building the same fine spirit of courage and devotion that characterized their activities upon the battle field. And their fight here proved anything but a "lost cause."

That these men were not unappreciative of the labors of "Yankees" who came among them when the city began to grow, is made obvious by the fact that many of these citizens subsequently were elevated to positions of preferment. The attitude of these Confederate veterans toward those who had worn the blue, and had served under the Stars and Stripes, is reflected in the following sentence, penned by Major Milner some years ago: "Among those who accepted our invitation to come to Birmingham were many members of the Grand Army of the Republic, and no better class of citizens are to be found anywhere. I wish we had more of them, and of their sons."

CHAPTER XXV

COMBINING LOANS WITH LAUGHTER

AS a rule, humor and banking are not associated, yet it is true that the founder of Birmingham's financial system was one of the greatest wits the city has ever known. Old-timers still chuckle over the waggish performances of Capt. Charles Linn, who established the first bank in the new-born community, and who demonstrated his faith in its future by erecting a three-story building of imposing architecture.

Diagonally across the street from this building a marsh had been converted into a park, and Capt. Linn caused a high flag-pole to be erected there. About this time three of the prominent men of the town had taken unto themselves wives, the list including Dr. Luman S. Handley, Capt. John

C. Henley and William Berney. Capt. Linn, ever zealous of the growth of the community, announced that he was going to fly his flag in honor of the first child born to these unions. And he did. Moreover, he raised it when the second child was born, and when the third came into the world. He raised it for the fourth, and the fifth, and again sent it up upon the advent of the sixth. Then, catching these fathers together one day, he said:

"Look here, boys, I'm going to call this thing off; you're about to wear my flag out!"

In celebration of his sixty-seventh birthday, forty years ago, Capt. Linn gave a community "party" in Linn Park, and several copies of the hand-bill which carried the announcement of the affair to the entire population, still are preserved. The events of the evening were set forth in numerical order, the last being as follows:

"7. Concluding with the eclipse of the moon, which will be seen shortly after 12 o'clock.

"In case of rain, the above will be postponed until the Monday following."

Happily, for observant astronomers in various parts of the country, it did not become necessary to postpone the eclipse.

The bank founded by Capt. Linn is today the largest in Birmingham, and one of the largest in the South. It was from the presidency of this institution that W. P. G. Harding, Governor of the Federal Reserve Board, was called to Washington.

The next financial institution, in point of size and age, is the Birmingham Trust, founded in the early days by a group of financiers which included William Rockefeller, a brother of John D. Rockefeller. The Rockefeller stock since has been acquired by local interests. This bank, now the largest bank in the State, is erecting a splendid new home as these lines are written.

The Traders National, the American Trust, and Steiner Brothers, are the other down-town banks. The latter was founded by B. Steiner, now of New York, who, while trying to do something for his own institutions many years ago, rendered a great service to the then struggling city. Coming into the possession of certain city bonds, behind which there was no security of special value, he had a constitutional amendment submitted by the legislature providing that Birmingham might levy a special tax of five mills to take care of the bonded indebtedness of the municipality incurred prior to 1901. This made his bonds gilt-edge securities, since the money derived from this tax brought in a very large sum, with the continued growth of the city. Normally, this tax would have expired with the maturity of the Steiner bonds, but it was made permanent by a subsequent amendment, and became applicable to all bonds of the city, whether issued in the past or at some time in the future.

This tax amounts today to more than $500,000 a year, and gives Birmingham a sinking fund for the payment of interest, and for the redemption of bonds, that places the credit of the municipality upon a high plane. It enables the city to pay off all bonds at maturity and to meet interest charges the moment they are due. Thus, an amendment passed years ago to protect a small issue of bonds has become the foundation of the city's financial strength.

The dean of Birmingham bankers is Colonel T. O. Smith, about whom one hears some interesting stories connected with certain inside happenings during the World War. During those times of doubt and uncertainty, the fires of patriotism burned brightly in this city, the great majority giving to the Nation the fullest measure of support. But there were a few whose allegiance was elsewhere, and they started out to make all the trouble they could for the community. Two great high school buildings were burned within forty-eight hours, and one of the largest grammar school buildings was set on fire, the loss running into thousands of dollars. It became evident that a campaign of terrorism had been launched by internal foes, and instantly there arose a demand for more adequate protection against this sinister element.

No publicity has ever been given the operations of the organization, but it is known that a society of vigilantes was organized and that it rendered services of incalculable value. The membership ran into hundreds, embracing the most representative men of the city, and it became a powerful adjunct to the law enforcement branches of the government, City, State and National. The campaign of terrorism was nipped in the bud, and shortly such terror as existed was in the hearts of the alien enemies and not in the breasts of patriotic citizens. Colonel Smith is credited with having been the directing head of this thoroughly effective organization, an organization that was ready instantly to respond to any call at any hour of the day or night, and without which there is no telling how far the alien enemy would have gone in his campaign of wantonness.

It is rather odd that a city as large as Birmingham should have only four banks in the downtown business section, but the absence of others may be accounted for by the fact that several large suburban communities have strong institutions of their own. Ensley, the great steel-making suburb, has two banks. There is one at Woodlawn, one at

North Birmingham, and another at Wylam. The North Birmingham bank, though a strong factor in the industrial life of the community, goes in for agricultural development, providing to farmers the means for obtaining fine stock for breeding purposes.

Building and loan associations are not so numerous in Alabama as they are in most states, and Birmingham has but three. These, however, are powerful institutions and have had an active part of these, the Alabama Home, has at its head a in the upbuilding of the community. The oldest man who, some years ago, hung up a record for saving that is unique. A boy of eighteen, W. V. M. Robertson, left the farm and went to Baltimore, where he worked for a year at $4.50 a week — and saved a part of this. The next year his salary was raised to $1,800, and, having taken a running start in the saving game, he kept up the pace by putting away $1,387 that second year. This sum formed the initial capital of a business that now runs into the millions. It is an actual fact that he has caused others to save millions of dollars and has been responsible for the erection of thousands of homes in and about this city.

This rather unusual case is cited because the theory seems to have gained ground that it requires huge sums of money to accomplish any-

REAR VIEWS OF HIGHLAND HOMES

thing big in this community. There are so many gigantic enterprises, with capital stock amounting to tens and hundreds of millions, that many young men appear to have conceived the notion that they cannot get anywhere unless they have large financial resources, forgetting that success is not in the multiplicity of dollars one has to manipulate, but is in the ability to keep at least a fractional part of each dollar, and to put that fraction to work.

There literally are thousands of prosperous citizens in this city whose prosperity began with the habit of thrift, and today, with a population that is growing with great rapidity, and with an ever increasing demand for things needed by the human family, the opportunities for men of small means were never more abundant. It requires vast sums to build and operate furnaces, mines and mills on the colossal scale that obtains in this district, but it requires very little to start a small shop, or store, or similar enterprise. I know a man who came here a few years ago and opened a modest retail store on what had become known as a "dead" corner. His establishment is one of the largest in the State today, and on January 1 he begins the erection of a building that will be the largest of its kind in the entire South. This man is L. Pitzitz.

Another huge mercantile establishment, known the country over, was started some years ago by a trio of young men, Lovemen, Joseph and Loeb, whose chief capital consisted of vision. Birmingham is full of examples of this character, each bearing witness to the fact that large results can be achieved from small beginnings.

Another illustration, in a somewhat different line, may not come amiss. A few years ago A. W. B. Johnson was running a small cafeteria, or lunch room, upon the top floor of his department store. Out of this incidental venture, conducted on a rather unusual basis, grew a "chain" idea which, when put into practice, grew amazingly.

Then there is the case of the three Blach brothers, who, from a small beginning, built up a great retail enterprise. Only a block away, the Saks brothers did the same thing, and the Jacobs brothers, on the same street, followed suit, as did the Burger brothers and the Caheen brothers—from which one might infer the brothers pull together here. R. D. Burnett, the smoke from whose cigars would look like a house afire if the daily output was consumed in a single spot, also started at the bottom. And there are innumerable others who have built similar enterprises upon a large scale.

In the industrial field, too, there are any number

of instances in which large fortunes have been created by individual initiative. Major E. M. Tutwiler, retired, came to Birmingham with the engineering crew of the Georgia Pacific Railroad, when that line was built into the city, and made a large fortune in the development of mining enterprises. Frank Nelson, Jr., started at the bottom in the same field and reached the top. One of the greatest lumber enterprises in the Southern States was built up by John L. Kaul from a modest beginning, his activities being largely responsible for the fact that Birmingham, though primarily an iron and steel center, is one of the leading lumber markets of the South. Several young men, like Thornton Estes, Mercer Barnett — typical figures among the newer generation — are headed in the same direction.

Ed. Barrett, once one of the right hand men to the great Henry Grady, of the Atlanta Constitution, came to Birmingham a generation ago and caught the Birmingham Age-Herald as it was tottering toward bankruptcy, and made it a highly profitable enterprise, doing it on sheer nerve. Victor Hanson, who grew up under Frank Glass, on the Montgomery Advertiser, gained control of the Birmingham News on the death of General Rhodes, and, with limited capital, made it one of the most prosperous papers in the country.

In every line of human endeavor, similar instances of triumphant success might be recorded, illustrating the fact that in Birmingham opportunity does not spend all its time pounding on the doors of those who have unlimited means.

Another interesting fact is that most of the directing heads of the great industrial enterprises in the Birmingham district are men who fought their way to the top. George Gordon Crawford, head of most of the subsidiary organizations of the United States Steel Corporation in Alabama, had no monetary advantage over thousands of other Georgia boys among whom he was reared; J. W. McQueen, Vice-President of the Sloss Company, worked his way from the bottom, and C. T. Fairbairn of the Republic Company, James Bowron of the Gulf States Steel Company, G. B. McCormack and Erskine Ramsay of the Pratt Consolidated Company, R. I. Ingalls of the Ingalls Iron Works, Harry Coffin of the Alabama Company, and numerous others, have attained topmost positions with giant organizations, because they had something in themselves, rather than something in the bank, when they started.

The ice and cold storage business has attained enormous proportions in the United States during the past twenty years, the growth in the South, where artificial ice is used exclusively, having been enormous, and one of the national figures in this development is a Birmingham man, W. J. Rushton. At the head of the ice manufacturers for years, he contributed as much as any one man to the growth of the industry at large, and built up a large number of enterprises of his own. He, too, started here on the lower rung of the ladder.

Birmingham is a city of warehouses, some of them attaining huge proportions, and the name on the greatest is that of "Harris." A poor farm boy, George C. Harris, came to this city and succeeded in making large plants grow where none had grown before.

G. T. Wofford, who had only limited resources a few years ago, went into business for himself, marketing a fuel mixture of his own invention. Today his filling stations are found all over the South, and the number is multiplying constantly.

Newsprint paper, by the way, soon will be manufactured in this district. Discovering vast quantities of spruce pine upon the mountains that parallel the Warrior River, E. W. Barrett conceived the idea that it might be suitable for making paper, and he caused a quantity of it to be sent to a big mill in the East, where it was converted into newsprint. The experiment was eminently successful, and Barrett used the product in getting out his newspaper here. Now plans for a large paper mill upon the Warrior are rapidly maturing and soon another "waste" product will be utilized.

Spruce pine long has been considered a worthless growth. Unlike the famous yellow pine of the South, it has no "heart" to speak of, being soft and having little power of resistance. The quality which renders it useless for building purposes makes it ideal for paper making—a discovery which promises to become the basis of another great industry.

In truth and soberness, it may be said that Alabama's industrial development is in its infancy, in spite of all that has been achieved during the past half century. New sources of wealth are being uncovered from time to time, while old sources become more productive, as their limitless extent is better understood. The deposits of iron ore, of coal, and of limestone and dolomite, the chief materials in steel making, are so vast that it will be many years before men need concern themselves about possible exhaustion. Not only so, but the sources of power for the utilization of these products are capable of being developed upon an enormous scale.

Muscle Shoals, where the United States Government spent nearly a hundred million dollars in the erection of air nitrate plants before work was suspended, is capable of being developed into one of the greatest sources of water power in the world. The Coosa River, whose energy now furnishes power to cities and towns in all parts of Alabama, is capable of much greater development, and there are numerous other sources of energy.

As this is written, Henry Ford is endeavoring to gain control of Muscle Shoals, and it is certain that the vast energy of those rapids will be developed if he comes into possession of the enterprise. Meanwhile the Alabama Power Company, which has one plant on the Coosa, producing 90,000 horse power, is adding to its developments upon that stream. It was this company that gave to the Government the Muscle Shoals site when the urgent need of nitrates arose during the war.

With its vast mineral deposits, with its extraordinary resources for the development of hydro-electric energy, and with its navigable rivers flowing to the Gulf, Alabama's future is assured. And Birmingham, the chief beneficiary of these natural gifts, should become one of the world's greatest centers of population, and thus fulfill to the utmost the vision of that little group of men who, fifty years ago, entered a barren waste and there laid the foundations of a great city.

-PIM-

Spotted something that isn't quite right?

Let us know and we'll fix it for future reprints.
And as a thank you for your diligence, we'll
send you a free Sothis book of your choice.

publisher@sothis.press

This page intentionally left blank

Made in United States
Orlando, FL
04 November 2026

90207239R00254